THE

REAL DIRT

ON AMERICA'S FRONTIER OUTLAWS

THE
REAL DIRT
ON AMERICA'S FRONTIER OUTLAWS

JIM MOTAVALLI

GIBBS SMITH
TO ENRICH AND INSPIRE HUMANKIND

This is for the women in my life—Mary Ann, Maya, and Delia—
and for frontier law enforcement, who had a tough time of it.

First Edition
24 23 22 21 20   5 4 3 2 1

Text © 2020 Jim Motavalli

Published by
Gibbs Smith
P.O. Box 667
Layton, Utah 84041

1.800.835.4993 orders
www.gibbs-smith.com

Designed by Devin Watson and Virginia Snow
Printed and bound in Hong Kong

Gibbs Smith books are printed on paper produced from sustainable PEFC-
certified forest/controlled wood source. Learn more at www.pefc.org.
Printed and bound in Hong Kong

Library of Congress Control Number: 2019948734

ISBN 13: 9781423654582

Front cover: A young Jesse James. (Library of Congress)

Page 2: The James Gang in full regalia, circa 1870, showing Frank and Jesse James, and Cole and Bob Younger. (Lordprice Collection/Alamy Stock Photo)

CONTENTS

PREFACE

Woody Guthrie had a soft spot for outlaws, but why try to redeem Pretty Boy Floyd? (Library of Congress)

There were at least two men who went by "Billy the Kid." In addition to the well-known Henry McCarty, Jr./William H. Bonney (who never actually called himself that, preferring "Kid Antrim") there was also Billy "The Kid" Burke. In the *1886 Professional Criminals of America*, he is profiled (via police files) as "one of the most adroit bank sneaks in America."

Burke, a native New Yorker like Bonney, was twenty-eight in 1886. He had a fairly simple, and definitely sneaky, way of working: while an associate created a disturbance out front, he'd slip into the director's office and snatch whatever was lying around. In 1881, he grabbed more than $10,000 at the Manufacturers Bank at Cohoes, New York. Of course—pursued by a bank clerk with a revolver—he dropped the money on the way out and was quickly captured.

Burke escaped and went west, but was easily recaptured in both Minneapolis and Cleveland. Maybe if he'd made it to the Wild West we'd remember *him* as Billy the Kid.

"Ladies love outlaws like babies love stray dogs," the 1972 Waylon Jennings song ("Ladies Love Outlaws") goes. Actually, Americans as a whole tend to romanticize outlaws, from Billy the Kid and "Pretty Boy" Floyd to Jack Henry Abbott (who committed murder *after* Norman Mailer helped free him) and

Rubin "Hurricane" Carter. The murderer/outlaw in Marty Robbins' big 1959 hit "El Paso" chooses to die for one last kiss.

Sample lyrics from Bentley Ball's 1919 "Jesse James" recording read:

> Jesse was a man, a friend to the poor.
> He'd never rob a mother or a child . . .
> He stole from the rich and he gave to the poor.
> He'd a hand and a heart and a brain.

In the song, even Jesse's kids are brave.

Woody Guthrie also wrote a song called "Jesse James," claiming to have run into him with some cowboys "on the old Dodge City trail." At least this one doesn't glorify the bandit, instead advising listeners who don't want to get filled with lead to "stay out of the badlands, where the red-hot bullets fly."

As glorified by Bob Dylan in the song "John Wesley Harding" (the singer's spelling of it), the outlaw:

> Was a friend to the poor
> He traveled with a gun in every hand
> All along this countryside
> He opened many a door
> But he was never known
> To hurt an honest man.

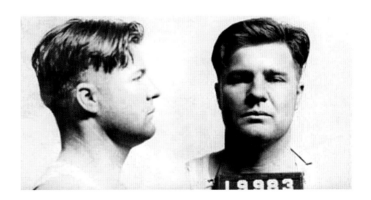

"Pretty Boy" Floyd has only the most dubious claim to Robin Hood status. (Wikipedia)

Dylan (who appeared non-memorably as "Alias" in the 1973 *Pat Garrett and Billy the Kid* film) was channeling his idol, Guthrie, when he uncovered J.W. Hardin. The source material was a Guthrie song claiming that the notorious "Pretty Boy" became an outlaw only after he defended his wife from "vulgar words of language" hurled by a deputy sheriff. After that, of course, "Every crime in Oklahoma was added to his name." And then in Guthrie's song, we get the myth of the outlaw as modern-day Robin Hood:

> Many a starvin' farmer
> The same old story told
> How the outlaw paid their mortgage
> And saved their little homes.

Bob Dylan and Joan Baez during the August 1963 March on Washington for Peace and Freedom. (Rowland Scherman/ National Archives)

C'mon, Floyd never did any such thing. He may have destroyed some mortgage documents in the banks he robbed, but that isn't confirmed. Paying someone's mortgage? Not likely! Obviously, Guthrie had social commentary on his mind. His "Pretty Boy" contains the wry couplet, "Some will rob you with a six gun / And some with a fountain pen." True enough, but he might have picked a better foil.

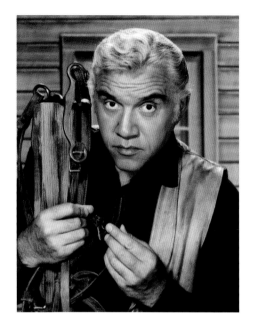

Lorne Greene on the Ponderosa during the filming of Bonanza. *His Ringo had "a spark of good." (Wikipedia)*

We like our outlaws to have "a spark of good" (as actor Lorne Greene intoned in his hit song "Ringo"), but it's hard to find redeeming factors in many of the men and women profiled in this book. They were vicious murderers, often killing for no reason, violent robbers of stage coaches and trains, and stock rustlers. There's a reason horse thieves were quickly hanged back then—it was a heinous crime.

Jesse James is remembered not for his racist views or his many murders, but for getting shot in the back by "the coward" Robert Ford. Butch Cassidy and the Sundance Kid (Harry Longabaugh) are fondly remembered because of the way they were portrayed by Robert Redford and Paul Newman in the movies, but in real life they had blood on their hands from many criminal enterprises.

Of course, as Luc Sante writes in his 1991 book *Low Life*, the enterprising young man of the nineteenth century, if he had the misfortune of being born poor or an immigrant to these shores, had the option of working in a store for a pittance and, maybe someday, owning one. On the other hand, he could become "a burglar, a footpad, a shoulder-biter, a gambling-house shill, a saloon runner, a swindler of immigrants, a poisoner of horses, a mayhem specialist for hire, a river pirate, a crimp, a dip, a ghoul. Then, with sufficient skill, and luck, and drive, and ferocity, he might come to lead his own gang." For women, the options were considerably fewer, including sweatshop labor or prostitution.

Some of the outlaws portrayed here were famous either in their own times or right after—James, Pearl Hart, Black Bart, Belle Starr. The dime novels and penny presses, usually without regard for accuracy, created their legends. Others, including Cassidy and Longabaugh, have Hollywood to thank for their fame. Concerning John Wesley Hardin, well, his star was dimming until Dylan plugged it back in.

Who remembers Cherokee Bill, the Bloody Espinosas, or Isom Dart today? There's an element of racism in the fact that the doings of African-American and Hispanic outlaws were rarely elevated to legend status in the national press (though they were infamous locally). But we don't much remember many white outlaws, such as Hoodoo Brown, Soapy Smith, or Belle Siddons, either. So, allow me to bring these memorable bad hats back to life.

As a way to put these outlaws' crimes in perspective, the Appall-o-Meter (which goes up to 10) judges them on the nature of their transgressions. The highest marks go to the "owlhoots" who killed in the greatest number, especially if their murders were completely senseless like killing someone because they were snoring.

BILLY THE KID

(1859-1881)

THE IRISH ENIGMA

APPALL-O-METER: 7

BILLY THE KID (AKA WILLIAM H. BONNEY OR HENRY MCCARTY, JR.)

Billy the Kid. (aka William H. Bonney, aka Henry McCarty, Jr.)
(Wikipedia)

THE LEGEND

As the deadliest outlaw the Old West ever produced, Billy the Kid had twenty-one notches in his pistol grip, one for each of the years he'd been alive. His first murder was at age twelve. Although a killer and a thief, the boyish Billy was personally friendly and likable, with a deep immersion in Mexican culture, which produced his girlfriend. There was a streak of good in him, and many of the verified killings occurred in the context of self-defense. He was a legendary escape artist and a deadly shot. He escaped the gallows, only to be shot during a cowardly ambush by Sheriff Pat Garrett in 1881. Things were changing in the West, and the people who made it colorful had to go.

HOW THEY GET IT WRONG

The Kid is remembered because he was a baby-faced teenager when he committed most of his crimes, and he died at age twenty-one, leaving few facts and a blank canvas on which to create a legend. His corpse wasn't even cold before the first biographies were published, with even the accounts based on eyewitness testimony filled with conjecture and made-up "facts."

Billy was shot on July 14, 1881, and by August 29, the Wide Awake Library had *The True Life of Billy the Kid* out for five cents. It manages to make errors in its second paragraph, proclaiming his actual name to have been "William McCarthy." It proclaims that "some have located his birthplace as the City of New York [where it actually did occur] but this is doubtless a mistake."

The True Life goes on to inform us that Billy's father brought the family to New Mexico, but dad was out of the picture early on. It was actually Billy's widowed mother who moved the family out West. They first lived in Indianapolis in the late 1860s, then went on to Wichita, Denver, Santa Fe (where she remarried), and then Silver City, where she died, leaving him an orphan at age fourteen.

The True Life has copious amounts of colorful Billy the Kid dialogue, no doubt mostly made up from whole cloth by the dime novel wordsmiths in New York. It states with full confidence that the Kid committed his first murder in Arizona at around age seventeen, gunning down Frank Douglass, his rival for the hand of the fair Senorita Quiseta. In reality, love was not at issue, and the person the Kid shot to death in 1877 was Frank "Windy" Cahill.

All of this is on the first two pages of *The True Life*. Pat Garrett's name is misspelled as "Garret," though Billy's bloody escape from his custody in Lincoln—the most famous moment in Kid lore, besides the death scene—is rendered with fair accuracy. And speaking of that death scene ("'Crack,' went Pat Garrett's rifle"), the book has it occurring on August 14 instead of July 14, possibly to make *The True Life*'s account seem more current. The book concludes, "Thus died the youngest and greatest desperado ever known in the world's history." That seems a bit thick. What about Genghis Khan?

One of the most interesting Billy the Kid books is Charles A. Siringo's *History of Billy the Kid*. Although not published until 1920, the book has some claim to authority on the subject. Siringo writes that he was "personally acquainted with [Billy], and assisted in his capture by furnishing Sheriff Pat Garrett with three of his fighting cowboys."

This book also claims that Billy was an outlaw "whose youthful daring has never been equaled in the annals of criminal history." It repeats the oft-cited myth that Billy "killed 21 men." But it adds, "Indians not included." Why not? The author quotes Billy as saying they "didn't count as human beings." *History* portrays Billy as a horrible racist, though it's difficult to separate his supposed sentiments from the tenor of the times.

IRISH ROOTS

Other bad actors with Irish roots include James "Whitey" Bulger, the Boston mobster (up to fifty dead in a long career); Emmett Dalton , of the train-robbing family, (see page 220)—he was the only survivor of the famous Coffeyville shootout in 1892; Jack "Legs" Diamond (originally Jack Moran, he was a noted bootlegger during Prohibition who survived a number of attempted hits); Owney "The Killer" Madden (another Prohibition-era New York gangster and onetime proprietor of the Cotton Club); and Charles Dean O'Banion (a rival of Al Capone).

And let's not forget, closer to the time under study, James Kirker, a fur trader born in County Antrim. A noted bigamist, he fought the Apaches for the bounty ($200 for men, $50 for women, $25 for children) and was allegedly responsible for taking the scalps of five hundred people. Much of his bloody work was in Mexico and, before he was declared *persona non grata* there, collaborated with some local thugs to murder one hundred-thirty law-abiding Apaches in Chihuahua. Kirker Pass in Contra Costa County, California, is named after him. Kirker died in 1852.

Myles Dungan, author of *How the Irish Won the West*, argues that Kirker would today be accused of "genocide or, at the very least, ethnic cleansing." Dungan asserts in his book that it was a man from Dublin who first raised the idea of cannibalism having taken place among the Donner Party, and that South Pass may have been discovered not by the famous American, Jedediah Smith, but rather by his lieutenant Thomas Fitzpatrick (born in County Cavan). Irish accents were definitely heard on the frontier.

This photo sometimes get represented as showing Billy at age 18, but though there is a resemblance, it probably isn't him. (Wikipedia)

WAS BILLY THE KID A RACIST?

Siringo says he got the following story directly from Billy the Kid's lips in 1878. When he was twelve, Billy traveled to Fort Union, New Mexico, to gamble with some African-American soldiers. There, he shot dead the (unnamed) "black nigger" who cheated him. The book says this killing occurred well before the murder of blacksmith Cahill, who is depicted as having insulted Billy's mother (actually, it was Billy himself who was the butt of cruel jokes). *History* says Cahill was stabbed three times, and Billy ran out of the saloon, "his right hand dripping with human blood." But Cahill was actually shot with a Colt .45.

History also has the Kid and some other desperadoes murdering a trio of Indians simply because they had a lot of valuable pelts and a dozen horses. "There was no fight. It was the softest thing I ever struck," Billy is quoted as saying.

The supposed murder of the African-American buffalo soldier occurs nowhere else in the Billy the Kid literature I've seen. Frankly, though it's supposedly first-hand from Billy himself, the murder seems as far-fetched as the florid dialogue in these accounts. He wasn't even arrested until he was fifteen when he stole from a Chinese laundry. It's ironic that the narratives from the actual period are much less reliable than those written one hundred years later.

The 1906 play *Billy the Kid* by Walter Woods was well received, running for twelve years in New York. It has Billy saying, "I roped seven niggers out of eight," to which ranch hand Con Handley replies with a gently admonishing, "Billy boy!"

Sheriff Pat Garrett "wrote" his own book, *The Authentic Life of Billy the Kid*, actually ghostwritten by itinerant journalist Ash Upson, and it came out in 1882. According to *True West*, it "failed to sell until years later, maybe because of the bad writing." Garrett himself made "no pretension to literary ability," but promised a "round, unvarnished tale," informed by his having known the Kid well before killing him. Unfortunately, this "faithful and interesting narrative" is plenty varnished, with a tendency to see the bright side of the Kid's actions. Was it guilt for shooting such a legendary figure?

It's Garrett's book that claims Billy killed his first victim defending a friend when he was twelve, and that the weapon was a knife. Off the young man went, "grasping a pocket-knife, its blade dripping with gore" and now "an outcast, a wanderer a murderer self-baptized in human blood."

The first kill was actually in 1877, in Arizona near Fort Grant, when Billy was sixteen or seventeen. And the victim, the Irish-born Cahill, had been giving the Kid grief about his youthful appearance and baby face. He called McCarty (by then calling himself Henry Antrim) a "pimp." McCarty responded by calling Cahill a "son of a bitch," and the fight was on. The Kid shot Cahill after the much bigger man got him pinned to the saloon floor. He then grabbed the fastest horse and rode off toward New Mexico, forever after a marked man.

Sheriff Pat Garrett wrote his own book on Billy the Kid, but it's no fount of accuracy. (Wikipedia)

Garrett's book also has the tale of the Kid murdering Indians for their goods. After they were shot, the book adds the detail that Billy the Kid called them three "good Injuns,"—good because they were dead. "No one regretted the loss of these Indians, and no money could be made by prosecuting the offenders," said Garrett.

The respected author Michael Ondaatje wrote *The Collected Works of Billy the Kid* in 1970, choosing to imagine how the young desperado might have lived. The title is ironic, since the collected works actually amount to a letter or two. The Kid could actually write fairly well, especially considering the times he lived in.

Using the Kid's voice, Ondaatje proclaims the death toll as follows:

> Morton, Baker, early friends of mine. Joe Bernstein. 3 Indians. A blacksmith when I was twelve, with a knife. 5 Indians in self defence (behind a very safe rock). One man who bit me during a robbery. Brady, Hindman, Beckwith, Joe Clark, Deputy Jim Carlyle, Deputy Sheriff J.W. Bell. And Bob Ollinger. A rabid cat [and] birds during practice.

BILLY IN STORY AND SONG

Billy the Kid is depicted in countless biographies, comic books, movies, and TV shows, with most of them being very inaccurate. He has been depicted on screen by Paul Newman, Kris Kristofferson, World War II hero Audie Murphy, Michael J. Pollard, Val Kilmer, and Emilio Estevez. Jane Russell played his fictional girlfriend in Howard Hughes' 1943 *The Outlaw*. The first Billy the Kid film was made in 1911, and there have been fifty since—most recently, *The Kid* (2019), with Dane DeHaan offering up a very plausible Billy. He's usually portrayed by much older actors.

At least they get it correct with the music, right? Wrong! "Ballad of Billy the Kid" by Billy Joel, on the *Piano Man* album, has an amazing number of inaccuracies (not to mention equine sound effects worthy of Ferde Grofé's "On the Trail"). The Kid wasn't born in Wheeling, West Virginia, he never robbed a bank (in Colorado or anywhere else), he actually had a sweetheart, and he most definitely didn't always ride alone—he was, on several occasions, a gang member.

Woody Guthrie's "Billy the Kid" (later also recorded by Ry Cooder) calls him "the boy bandit king," and repeats the idea of him killing twenty-one men—the first at twelve. "Sheriff Pat Garrett will make 22," it said. But at least the song doesn't glorify and excuse a vicious outlaw, as Guthrie did with his "Pretty Boy Floyd." Aaron Copland's ballet "Billy the Kid" has our hero turning into an outlaw after his mother is killed by a stray bullet during a gunfight. He stabs the murderer, then—a tragic figure—goes on the lam.

WHAT WE ACTUALLY KNOW

The evidence suggests that Henry McCarty was born in an Irish neighborhood in Manhattan around 1859. Records on file at Saint Peter's Church, in what is now the Financial District of Manhattan, reflect the baptism of someone by that name, born September 17 as the son of Patrick (or Michael) McCarty and Catherine Devine McCarty, on September 28, 1859. The parents, reportedly refugees from the Irish potato famine, were also married in the church in 1851. McCarty may not have been young Henry's father.

Very little is known about young Henry's early years. He may well have learned Irish along with English, as his neighborhood would have been intensely Irish, with

George Catlin's painting "Five Points" from 1827 depicts a neighborhood, home to many Irish-Americans, that the New York Herald *said in 1858 was a "nest of drunkenness, roguery, debauchery, vice, and pestilence." (Metropolitan Museum of Art/ Wikipedia Commons)*

many Irish-born speakers of that language. In the 1870s, according to IrishCentral.com, the Kid was said to have been pressed into service in New Mexico to translate for a woman named Mary, the niece of an Irishman named Pat Coughlan, who could speak only Irish.

Garrett's *Authentic Life*, which is oddly admiring, reports that Billy had little recollection of his father, who was gone from the family and possibly dead by the time Billy, his mother, two brothers, and a sister settled in New Mexico after a mid-1860s stopover in Indianapolis. The city directories in Indianapolis for 1867 and 1868 list Catherine as Michael's widow.

Billy was "the darling of his young companions in his gentler moods, and their terror when the angry fit was on him," Garrett's biography states.

The young man showed a precocious talent for partying and dancing, as well as for gambling. "He became adept at cards and was noted among his comrades as successfully aping the genteel vices of his elders," Garrett reports.

The widow Catherine McCarty had met an Indiana Civil War veteran named William Antrim in 1865 and kept company with him. The family, with Antrim, lived for a time in Wichita, Kansas. Catherine started a laundry business there but contracted tuberculosis and found it necessary to move her family out of the city to Santa Fe, New Mexico (after a period in Denver). She married Antrim at the First Presbyterian Church in Santa Fe in March of 1873.

Catherine was now ill with tuberculosis. Antrim wasn't much good at stepping into the breach. He was an indifferent stepfather, and Billy was left mostly to his own devices. Garrett says that Antrim's "tyranny and cruelty" drove him from home.

BILLY GOES BAD

The Kid's criminal life evidently started in Santa Fe, but the ever-sympathetic Garrett notes, "It has been said that at this tender age [Billy] was convicted of larceny in Santa Fe, but as a careful examination of the court records of that city fail to support the rumor, and as Billy, during all his after life, was never charged with a little meanness or petty crime, the statement is to be doubted."

The family moved to Silver City, New Mexico, where an ailing Catherine took in boarders. Billy attended school for a brief time, but according to *American Heritage* "[Silver City's] busy streets, saloons and dance halls were more to his liking." Catherine couldn't be a steadying influence—she died in the fall of 1874. Antrim "farmed the boys out—and kept farming them out," writes Mark Lee Gardner.

A life of crime was not preordained, but after young Billy became an orphan, his name did indeed start to show up in the police logs for petty theft (of butter, for instance), and with the street-tough companion George Schaefer (known as "Sombrero Jack") of shirts, blankets, and guns lifted from a Chinese laundry. Billy's landlord reported him to the police, and he was thrown into jail in Silver City. But he escaped through the chimney flue and hightailed it out of town. Horse theft charges followed. It was soon after this that Billy shot Cahill in Arizona and headed back to New Mexico.

As he lay dying, Cahill gave an amazingly objective account of what had happened. "I had some trouble with Henry Antrem [sic], otherwise known as Kid, during which he shot me. I had called him a pimp and he called me a son of a bitch; we then took hold of each other; I did not hit him, I think; saw him go for his pistol and tried to get hold of it, but could not and he shot me in the belly."

Now a wanted man, it's likely that the Kid abandoned the Henry McCarty/Antrim name and became William Bonney around this time. He was apparently already The Kid, as Cahill pointed out.

Irish-born John Henry Tunstall helped set off the Lincoln County War. (Wikipedia)

THE LINCOLN COUNTY WAR

The cattle center of Lincoln County, New Mexico—at almost 30,000 square miles—was the biggest in the U.S. at that time. The big money to be made via government contracts to provision Fort Stanton were controlled by a syndicate (J.J. Dolan and L.G. Murphy were the principals) operating a general store known as "the House." Challenging their hegemony were John Henry Tunstall (English) and Alexander McSween (Scottish). The Kid came back to New Mexico and promptly took a side—the losing one, as it turned out—in the Lincoln County War, starting in 1878.

Tunstall earned the enmity of Dolan and Murphy when he challenged the House by opening his own general store in Lincoln.

Tensions increased, and Tunstall hired some young gun thugs—including the newly minted William Bonney (who had recently taken up with some cattle rustlers known as "The Boys")—to serve as protection. The sides seemed fluid; "The Boys" had earlier worked for the House.

Tunstall and Billy the Kid had become close quite quickly, with the former proclaiming (at least according to Bill O'Reilly's *Legends and Lies*), "That's the finest lad I ever met. He's a revelation to everyday and would do anything to please me. I'm going to make a man out of that boy yet."

The House turned up some charges against Tunstall and then went to his door to enforce a court order. The House posse retreated, but when Tunstall, evidently a brave man, rode up to them to protest their presence on his land, he was shot dead. "Although he had not worked for Tunstall long, Billy the Kid deeply resented this cold-blooded murder, and he immediately began a vendetta of violence against The House and its allies," the *History Channel* said. "Lincoln County became a war zone, and both sides began a spree of vicious killings," the report said. The Kid allegedly said, "I'll get every son of a bitch who helped kill John if it's the last thing I ever do." And so the fighting continued until 1884.

The Kid and other Tunstall devotees founded The Regulators, and went after The House guerrilla-style. Their victims, with The Kid's six-shooter in the mix, included Frank Baker, Buck Morton, and William McClosky (a Regulator who was accused of spying for The House). They were gunned down at Blackwater Creek, with the Regulators claiming that Baker and Morton had killed McClosky and died trying to escape. These were three more notches for Billy the Kid, whether he fired the fatal shots or not.

One of the Kid's victims was the corrupt Sheriff William Brady, a native-born Irishman from County Cavan. (Wikipedia)

That same year, 1878, the Regulators also killed the corrupt Ireland-born Sheriff William Brady, after ambushing him and shooting him a dozen times from behind an adobe wall. Brady's deputy George Hindman was also shot, but not by Billy, who was wounded in the melee. Brady was victim number five.

It may seem that the Kid was only getting started, but he was actually winding down. The Lincoln County War—and the killing of Sheriff Brady—had made Billy a big "get" for law enforcement. Apparently for love, he chose not to flee to Mexico, where his familiarity with the culture and fluent Spanish could have cushioned his exile.

The new sheriff to replace Brady was George "Dad" Peppin, and he put together a large force to bring the Kid in, condition unimportant. Peppin, too, was a House sympathizer.

Lincoln County, New Mexico Sheriff George "Dad" Peppin was known to bend the law. This is his last-known photograph. (Wikipedia)

The posse, with the aid of U.S. troops under the command of Lieutenant Colonel Nathan Augustus Monroe Dudley, surrounded McSween's residence in July of 1878. Billy was inside the large house (described as a mansion) with fourteen companions. Fierce fighting erupted and continued for five days. During a lull, Billy was asked to surrender for Brady's murder. The Peppin forces said a warrant was in hand. "We, too, hold warrants for you and your gang, which we will serve on you, hot from the muzzles of our guns," Billy supposedly replied (as reported in Siringo's *History of Billy the Kid*), though the quote sounds so much like cheap melodrama that it is probably fictitious.

Firing continued, and the mansion was soon pockmarked with bullets. Dudley threatened to use his two cannons on the house. Two of the attackers, Robert Beckwith and John Jones, tried to get into the house via the rear kitchen door and were met with a fusillade from the Kid, killing Beckwith and wounding Jones. Bonney and his men then exited through that same door and got away across the river behind the house. McSween, refusing to abandon his own house, was shot nine times and killed.

The whole Lincoln County War, which killed twenty-two people, was embarrassing for President Rutherford B. Hayes, who installed Lew Wallace (a Civil War general who later wrote the bestselling *Ben-Hur: A Tale of the Christ*) as New Mexico's territorial governor. An amnesty was offered, but it exempted men like Billy who'd been charged with murder. Thinking strategically, the Kid thought he could gain his freedom if he offered eyewitness testimony to the murder of McSween's attorney, Huston Chapman. He wrote to the new governor, saying he would lay down his arms if pardoned. "I have no wish to fight any more indeed I have not raised an arm since your proclamation [of amnesty]," Billy wrote.

"I have authority to exempt you from prosecution, if you will testify to what you say you know," Wallace wrote to the fugitive. Wallace and William Bonney did indeed meet, on March 17, 1879, and two days later Billy surrendered and was jailed and loosely guarded in the back of a store. He did testify about the murder of Chapman, but he wasn't pardoned. In fact, he was indicted for killing Sheriff Brady.

It's hardly surprising that rather than wait to be tried and hung, he escaped—not to Mexico, but to Fort Sumner, New Mexico, where he was sweet on Paulita Maxwell. *True West* reports that Maxwell may have become pregnant by the Kid. She did have a daughter, who died at age 16. But Maxwell denied, in a 1920s interview, having had an affair with young Billy—though she admitted to being infatuated with him.

BILLY AND JESSE?

Also in dispute is whether, around 1879, Billy the Kid met Jesse James. The claim is made in a 1920s book, *A Frontier Doctor*, by Dr. Henry F. Hoyt, who knew Bonney and worked at the Exchange Hotel in Las Vegas, New Mexico, that year. James claimed to be "Mr. Howard from Tennessee," and Billy said he was offered a job as a train robber, but declined because it wasn't his form of criminal endeavor.

A photo supposedly taken in Las Vegas that year is purported to show young Billy with Jesse James and Doc Holliday, but its provenance is weak. The men in the photo are not wearing their six-guns.

In Fort Sumner on January 10, 1880, the Kid got into an altercation in Bob Hargrove's saloon with a reportedly obnoxious fellow who went by the name of "Texas Red" Joe Grant, who'd been bragging around town that he was tougher than the famous and very much wanted Bonney. After Red reportedly tried to kill him, Bonney dispatched the upstart with a bullet in the face.

This one's a bit fuzzy, but it is popularly believed to be murder number six. Reports *True West*, "Some scholars debate whether the Grant fight actually took place…[T]he details of the shooting became part of the folklore around Fort Sumner and the 'facts' in the case are mighty slim. Still, the fight has the ring of truth to many Billy scholars and is generally accepted as being a bona fide event."

Fuzziness was Billy's stock in trade. Also, in 1880, according to Mark Lee Gardner's *To Hell on a Fast Horse*, he told census taker Lorenzo Labadie that his real name was William Bonney, and that he was twenty-five years old (giving him an 1855 birth date). He also said he was born in Missouri to parents who were also born there. It's unlikely he was ashamed of his Irish roots; more likely he was trying to cover up his trail of crime.

Pat Garrett was getting more interested in capturing Billy the Kid. The pair knew each other and possibly posed together in a recently unearthed photograph. Accounts differ as to whether they knew each other well, but some say they had been frequent gambling buddies. Garrett became the Lincoln County sheriff in 1880. His first order of business: capturing the Kid, who had a $500 reward on his head.

The Kid could claim to have been acting out of self-defense, loyalty, or friendship in some of his crimes, but he degenerated into a common horse and cattle thief, working with a gang known as "The Rustlers." The Kid's gang got surrounded by a force led by deputy Will Hudgens, but once again escaped in a melee that cost the life of Jimmy Carlyle, a well-respected figure. The Kid didn't shoot him, but he got blamed for it.

Now the public really wanted the Kid's blood, and Garrett was on his trail. This was bad. Michael Ondaatje, in his imagined life of Bonney, has him saying of Pat Garrett, "[He] had the ability to kill someone on the street, walk back and finish a joke." The sheriff succeeded in making it hot for him, killing one gang member, Tom O'Folliard, and then trapping the gang in an old stone building. After he surrendered, the Kid told the *Las Vegas Gazette* that if they'd continued the siege they'd have eventually starved to death. "I thought it was better to come out and get a good square meal," he said.

The Kid was undoubtedly lying when he told the paper, "I haven't stolen any stock. I made my living by gambling but that was the only way I could live. They wouldn't let me settle down; if they had I wouldn't be here today."

The Kid was convicted of murdering Sheriff Brady and sentenced to be hanged in Lincoln on May 13, 1881. After his trial, he told the *Mesilla News* that his advice was "never to engage in killing." But he still thought he deserved a pardon from Governor Wallace. According to the paper, he said:

> Considering the active part Wallace took on our side and the friendly relations that existed between him and me, I think he ought to pardon me. Don't know that he will do it. When I was arrested for that murder, he let me out and gave me freedom of the town and let me go about with my arms. When I got ready to go, I left. Think it hard that I should be the only one [involved in the Lincoln County War] to suffer the extreme penalties of the law.

Kris Kristofferson as the Kid and Bob Dylan as "Alias" in Pat Garrett and Billy the Kid *(1973). The Kid guns down a bunch of people in just one scene.*

Dane Dehaan as Billy the Kid, after Ethan Hawke's Pat Garrett gets the drop on him. (Lionsgate)

BILLY ON FILM

America never tires of the story of Billy the Kid. Actor Dane DeHaan, who plays him in *The Kid* (2019), describes young Bonney as "an awesome character to play." His *Build* interviewer calls Billy "a psycho" and "a product of his times" (whatever that means). DeHaan replies that the outlaw was "a victim of the news cycle—everyone knew who Billy the Kid was because he was always in the news. He was a legend, and everyone had these preconceived notions about him. What we tried to do in the film is depict events that actually occurred in his life and say, 'Who was this guy really? Why did he do what he was doing?'" Of course, the film doesn't really answer that question. Billy the Kid will forever be an enigma.

DeHaan's is actually the best portrayal of Billy the Kid I've seen, in part because he captures the ambiguities of the fellow—a murderer, yes, but also a lover and (despite his apparent, or at least alleged, racism) an internationalist who was said to speak three languages and appreciate Mexican culture. He didn't shoot *everybody* he came across. The film shows him holding his fire occasionally. "He didn't always want to hurt people, but the Wild West was a rough place," DeHaan said, adding that in earlier portrayals he was often seen as "this suave character, which is not what he was at all."

BILLY'S BLOODY ESCAPE AND DEATH

Considering how often the Kid had escaped from captivity, you'd think he would have been heavily guarded, but this was not the case. He was chained up in the second story of a downtown building in Lincoln but taken out for meals and to use the outhouse facilities. His guards were Bob Olinger (a nemesis from the Lincoln War) and Deputy James W. Bell.

Escorted down the stairs, the Kid knocked his guard down and, grabbing a pistol that may have been stashed for him, killed Bell (who made it out of the building and collapsed on the street, in classic Western style). Olinger heard the shots and came running back, only to meet with the Kid holding his own shotgun. "Hello, old boy!," Mark Lee Gardner's *To Hell on a Fast Horse*, quotes him as saying before he let the lawman have it with both barrels. These were murders seven and eight, and as far as we know, the last ones committed by Billy the Kid.

The rest is anticlimactic. The Kid did not die with gun in hand. He hung around Fort Sumner, and the following July Garrett got wind that his quarry might be staying at a ranch with Pete Maxwell, brother of Paulita.

The scene is recounted in Garrett's 1920 biography. Garrett claims the Kid had gone that night to the home of a Mexican friend, where he "pulled off his hat and boots, threw himself on a bed, and commenced reading a newspaper." Later, he got hungry, telling a friend there, "Give me a butcher knife and I will go over to Pete [Maxwell]'s and get some beef; I'm hungry."

At precisely the same time, Garrett had gone to Maxwell's house, found him asleep, and was sitting on the bed asking about the Kid's whereabouts. "At that moment, a man sprang quickly into the door, looking back, and called twice in Spanish, 'Quien es'? [Who is it?]…He came on in. He was bareheaded. From his step I could perceive he was either barefooted or in his stocking feet, and held a revolver in his right hand and a butcher knife in his left."

Young Billy shoots a bartender in 1880. The wood engraving is from the lurid Police Gazette. *(Everett Collection Historical/ Alamy Stock Photo)*

Maxwell whispered to Garrett, "That's him." The Kid raised his pistol, but Garrett was quicker. "I drew my revolver and fired, threw my body aside, and fired again," Garrett wrote. "The second shot was useless; the Kid fell dead. He never spoke. A struggle or two, a little strangling sound as he gasped for breath, and the Kid was with his many victims." The first shot went in just above the heart. Garrett's aides had seen the bareheaded man enter the house, but "hearing his hail in excellent Spanish, they naturally supposed him to be a Mexican."

The contemporary obituaries are interesting. The *New York Sun*, under the headline "Desperado Dies in Western Gun Play," described Mr. Bonney as "the scourge of the southwest," and claims that the Kid had been intent on murdering Maxwell and that Pat Garrett's quick action saved his life. "Bonney, who was born in Brooklyn [sic], had slain 21 men [sic] and was 21 years old when Garrett's shot ended his fiendish career."

The Daily Graphic vastly inflated the Kid's criminal enterprise, proclaiming that he had "built up a criminal organization worthy of the underworld of any of the European capitals. He defied the law to stop him and he stole, robbed, raped [sic], and pillaged the countryside until his name became synonymous of the grim reaper himself." The headline: "Desperado Trapped in Lair of Luxury."

Within a year, there were no less than eight spurious novels about the life and bad times of Billy the Kid on the market.

BILLY THE KID MYSTERIES

Given the Kid's notoriety, it's not surprising that claims of his survival into old age would be made. In 1948, a paralegal named William V. Morrison heard that an elderly gentleman named Ollie "Brushy Bill" Roberts in Hico, Texas, claimed to have been William Bonney—and still wanted that official pardon. Morrison met Roberts and filed a petition on his behalf, but Roberts died just a month later.

Another claimant was John Miller, who died in 1937 and is buried in Prescott, Arizona. To help settle these claims, around 2003, there was a groundswell of interest in digging up the Kid's remains and DNA testing them. It didn't happen. The course of action was to test Brushy Bill's body and that of the body in the Kid's New Mexico grave against the remains of Catherine Antrim, the Kid's mother. But all the grave markers in the Fort Sumner cemetery disappeared in a 1904 flood. The whereabouts of the Kid's actual remains, and that of his mother, are unknown.

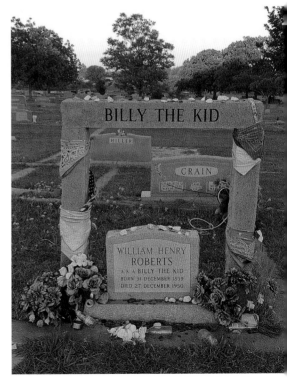

Top: Brushy Bill Roberts came forward claiming to be Billy the Kid. Tests were inconclusive, and the governor of New Mexico rejected the claim at Roberts' death in 1950. (Wikipedia)

Bottom: Brushy Roberts' grave site certainly makes the case that the man was Billy the Kid. (Wikipedia)

Top: Did Billy the Kid play croquet? Apparently so. This photograph ($2 at a flea market in 2010) was authenticated by National Geographic, and is reported to show the entire Regulators, at the 1878 wedding of one of their number, Charlie Bowdre. (Courtesy Randy Guijarro)

Bottom: The uncropped wedding photograph, showing the Regulators at play. (Courtesy Randy Guijarro)

Opposite: This 1880 tintype, unearthed in 2011 (at a flea market for $10), is believed to show Billy the Kid (second from right) and Sheriff Pat Garrett (extreme left) taken in 1880. (Courtesy Frank Abrams)

The only other mystery is that of the photographs. For ages, it was believed that only one image existed. But a second photo, which shows William Bonney, in a distinctive hat, and his Regulator friends playing croquet after a wedding in New Mexico in 1878, was valued at five million dollars in 2015. It was found in a cardboard box with other photos in a junk shop in Fresno, California, in 2010. Collector Randy Guijarro paid $2 for it.

The third photo is a tintype of five men in western garb, dug up at a flea market in 2011 by North Carolina lawyer Frank Abrams (who paid $10 for it). It is believed to have been taken between 1875 and 1880 and shows both Billy the Kid and Pat Garrett. This reinforces the idea that they were gambling friends, known as "Big Casino" and "Little Casino."

Top: Frederick Wadsworth Loring was no Billy the Kid. (Wikipedia)

Bottom: Songwriter Steve Tilston wasn't thinking about Billy the Kid when he wrote "Slip Jigs and Reels," but it fits. (Wikipedia)

THE POWER OF THE GUN

The song I consider the best about Billy the Kid, "Slip Jigs and Reels" by the English singer-songwriter Steve Tilston, is not even actually about him. Tilston told me he made up the story of an Irish-born minor desperado in the West. The inspiration was a picture he'd seen in Santa Fe of the very real Frederick Wadsworth Loring, who was killed by Indians in 1871. Tilston said, "The Billy the Kid myth is very potent and you're not the first to think my song is about him, I suppose it unintentionally adds to the myth. Books, ballads and films are not usually made about the comings and goings of the good guys."

In the song, a young man sails to New York with a ten-shilling note sewn into the lining of his grandfather's coat. He gets into a terrible fight, a man lies dead, and he flees west with "one eye open, a six-gun in bed." Crossing the plains where the buffalo roam, he "dreams of the mountains and green fields of home." He retains a fondness for the Irish dances immortalized in the song's title. They called him "The Kid," and by twenty-one, "All that he knew was the power of the gun." By twenty-three, he'd killed five men who "got in his way as he rambled around." When the Indians ambush him, the ten-shilling note is still sewn into the coat's lining.

Amazingly enough, young Billy actually gave this same explanation for why he killed so many people, at least according to the 1881 *True Life*. Asked in the text why he killed a fellow named McCluskey, the "young monster" replies, "He was in the way."

Tilston said he didn't know much about the actual Loring when he wrote the song, but that true tale is worthy of the silver screen, too. Loring was a minor playwright and journalist in Boston, a Harvard graduate, and a friend of James Russell Lowell. He might have become a major figure had he not accepted an assignment to accompany a surveying excursion to Arizona led by Lieutenant George M. Wheeler.

Loring turned in a few poorly regarded stories about the expedition, and then he was killed with five other members of the troupe by Yavapai Indians in what was known as the Wickenburg Massacre. Loring's work was posthumously immortalized in poetry anthologies.

Tell me, doesn't "Slip Jigs and Reels" tell more of Billy the Kid's story than Frederick Wadsworth Loring's? Henry McCarty certainly could have been born in Ireland. What might his voice have sounded like? A bit like Dane DeHaan's in *The Kid*, I would wager, or Daniel Day Lewis' transatlantic Bill "The Butcher" Cutting in *Gangs of New York* (set in the same period). The Kid was said to have been fluent in the Irish language.

WHEN THEY WENT BAD

With the Kid, the critical moment would seem to have been when he became an orphan, around 1874. He already had a string of robberies assigned to him (a tub of butter taken from a rancher), but he was reportedly an intelligent and plucky young man who could have made an honest living. As we have learned, though, he didn't.

WHAT THEY SAID

Criminals tend to justify their actions or claim they are innocent of the charges against them. Nobody in a prison is guilty, their guards say. Bonney, who was well known as a cattle and horse thief (but never robbed a bank or held up a stagecoach), claimed, "I never stole any stock." He told the *Las Vegas Gazette*, "They wouldn't let me settle down; if they had I wouldn't be here today." In other words, he'd have gone straight if given half a chance. But the facts, skimpy as they are, tell a different story.

As quoted in the book *The West*, Bonney was asked why he appeared to take it easy, even when in custody. "What's the use of looking at the gloomy side of everything?" he said. "The laugh's on me this time."

BLACK BART

(1829-1888)

A GENTLEMAN BANDIT

APPALL-O-METER: 4

BLACK BART
(AKA CHARLES E. BOLES)

Charles E. Boles lived the high life as a dandy in San Francisco off his ill-gotten gains as the notorious Black Bart. (Wiki Commons)

THE LEGEND

According to the 1948 *It's an Old California Custom* by Lee Shippey, Black Bart was the most successful stagecoach robber who ever lived, and his legend lives on in a thousand "oaters," which is what *Variety* called westerns during their heyday.

Shippey admired Bart as "the standout among the Gold Rush bandits." Here he was, an older guy always working alone, always on foot, and yet somehow besting heavily armed guards and getting away with the treasure—twenty-seven out of twenty-eight times.

The ambush, the shotgun held by a man in a long coat, the driver offering no resistance and throwing down the box, the poems left at the scene, the chivalrously treated passengers (unless the gunman is a real bad hat)—it's all part of the Black Bart legacy. The Danish band Volbeat would like to see him rise from his grave to maraud once more. This is from their noisy metal song, "Black Bart":

> Rise Black Bart, rise I'm calling
> Calling your spirit out
> Dust off your hat and hatchet
> There are boxes out there with your name and mark.

HOW THEY GET IT WRONG

The mysterious outlaw Black Bart was initially considered a scary guy. This is from a contemporary wanted poster circa 1877, offering a reward of "$1,000 in gold coin: This dastardly villain cunningly conceals himself in a long linen duster—artfully using a flour sack with eyeholes over his head."

Wanted: a horse-less man in a long coat with a rusty shotgun.

But Black Bart's case is one where the truth is just as strange as the fiction, and his reality was odder than any stories made up during his brief reign of crime. He really *did* leave poems at the scene of his holdups, and the doggerel wasn't half bad. And who wasn't surprised when the fearsome bandit was revealed to be the mild-mannered and elegantly dressed Charles Boles, who wore a derby hat and carried a cane? He had been a well-respected citizen of San Francisco for years. He told people he was "in mining" and looked and acted like a successful businessman.

Far from escaping on the thundering hooves of a trusted steed, he committed his robberies on foot—he was afraid of horses. According to Mark McLaughlin's *Black Bart: Stage Robber,* "He was skinny, short and bald, and didn't even own a horse. He walked to his crimes, carrying a shotgun so old and rusty that it wouldn't shoot. In fact, the weapon was never loaded."

Still, there was likely some embellishment in the story of Black Bart. After all, he only left poems at two of his crimes. During his first robbery in 1875, did he really order driver John Shine to throw down his strongbox, then shout, "If he dares to shoot, give him a solid volley, boys"? According to this story, Shine saw rifle barrels poking out from the bushes and didn't want to get peppered with lead. He threw down that box (with $160 aboard). After Bart left, the rifles were discovered to be sticks placed there by the solo robber. It's a good story, anyway.

WHAT WE ACTUALLY KNOW

Charles E. Boles, the man who would become Black Bart, was born in Norfolk, England, around 1829, decamping with his family (who spelled the name "Bowles") to Jefferson County, in upstate New York, two years later. He could have settled down on the farm, but like many young men at the time, he got gold fever in 1849 when he was twenty and headed for California with his cousin, David. The pair mined the north fork of the American River but didn't make a success of it and went back East in 1852.

Not admitting defeat, Charles and David, with Charles' brother Robert in tow, returned to California. Both David and Robert got sick and died soon after arriving in the Golden State. Charles did some more mining, without success, and returned home—soon heading to Illinois, where (now spelling his name "Boles") he married Mary Elizabeth Johnson in 1854. The couple had four children.

The Civil War changed many lives, including that of Charles Boles, who volunteered at Decatur for the 116th Regiment of the Illinois Infantry. Boles distinguished himself in the Union Army, and in 1864, was seriously wounded in combat. According to BlackBart.com, "Considering the conditions of the wound [in his right side and abdomen] it is remarkable that he survived." But survive he did, and returned to the field for further combat in Atlanta where he reportedly took part in Sherman's March to the Sea. He was a sergeant (after serving as a brevet lieutenant) when he was mustered out in 1865.

Boles went home to Illinois and got behind the plow, but he doesn't seem to have taken to the farm life any better in the Midwest than he did in New York. Once again he headed out to look for gold, this time landing in Montana, near Butte. He operated a mine with a partner named Henry Roberts, paying $200 in gold dust for the claim. Unfortunately, he refused a buyout offer from some men connected to Wells Fargo and Company, and they responded by cutting off the water supply he needed to locate his gold. Boles vowed revenge and claimed in a letter home that he was going to "take steps." He did!

BECOMING BLACK BART

Instead of returning home in 1871, as he told his wife he was going to do, Boles headed for San Francisco where he morphed into the about-town man of means and mining, Charles E. Boles. A lavish lifestyle that included high-hat hotels, fine dining, and the best in tailored clothing ensued, paid for by robbing stagecoaches as the bandit Black Bart.

The name "Black Bart" probably came from a serial novel contemporary to Boles' time, *The Case of Summerfield*, by William Henry Rhodes, first published in 1871. Black Bart is the name adopted by one Bartholomew Graham, a former lieutenant in the Confederate Army, serving under Generals Sterling Price and the fearsome guerrilla leader William Clarke Quantrill. A $10,000 reward was put on the all-in-black Graham's (Black Bart) head for murder. He was also suspected, in a case of art influencing real life, of robbing the Wells Fargo stage at Grizzly Bend.

"He was a man originally of fine education, plausible manners and good family, but strong drink seems early in life to have overmastered him, and left him but a wreck of himself," the book says. It goes on to state:

> But he was not incapable of generous or, rather, romantic acts; for, during the burning of the Putnam House in this town last summer, he rescued two ladies from the flames. In so doing he scorched his left hand so seriously as to contract the tendons of two fingers, and this very scar may lead to his apprehension. There is no doubt about his utter desperation of character, and, if taken at all, it will probably be not alive.

Of course, there was also another, much earlier Black Bart: a Welsh-speaking pirate named Bartholomew Roberts who died in 1722. He was a formidable foe, second only to the legendary Captain Morgan as a military and political organizer. But he posed a danger to the British crown, and his freebooting days were brief.

It was actually a laundry mark that led to the arrest of Boles' Black Bart persona, a man who was anything but desperate of character and in fact never fired the shotgun he

carried. Even the wanted poster noted that he appeared to be "a man of gentle birth with the manners of a perfect gentleman." He was no excitable youth; Boles was forty-six in 1875 when the first robbery occurred.

And although he fought on the Union side, not the Confederate, Boles fits Rhodes' Black Bart profile quite well. He did come from a good family and had "plausible" manners, and he was indeed capable of generous and romantic acts. One stage guard said that Boles admired his gun, and paid him $50 for it—instead of just taking it. He was especially nice to the women he encountered and returned their jewelry and cash. To one such female passenger who was attempting to climb out and hand over her valuables, he reportedly said, "No, lady, don't get out. I never bother the passengers. Keep calm. I'll be through here in a minute and on my way."

It's an Old California Custom reports that "Bart never killed anyone. Indeed, he never even hurt anyone.…All he wanted was the Wells Fargo box and the mail. In 28 robberies, he never fired a shot."

Mark McLaughlin has said, "Bart's strategy was deceptively simple psychology. He would wait at a dangerous bend in the road where the stage was forced to creep along slowly. At just the right moment, he emerged as an apparition in the deepening twilight."

The first robbery was July 26, 1875, and Black Bart held up the aforementioned Wells Fargo driver John Shine in Calaveras County (where Mark Twain's frogs had their jumping contest) at Funk Hill, between Copperopolis and Milton. Shine heard a polite bandit with a deep voice proclaim, "Throw down the box." Undoubtedly, he looked fearsome in his long linen duster and Klan-like flour sack mask, though it was mostly an illusion. It was the gang of one who couldn't shoot straight.

In December, Black Bart struck again, this time in Yuba County, four miles from Smartville. Driver Mike Hogan threw down that box. It was probably smart that our pedestrian robber moved around a lot, since it was hard to get a bead on him. In the first four robberies, he stepped out of the bushes in four different counties.

POETRY MAN

It was on August 3, 1877, during the fourth robbery (between Point Arenas and Duncan's Mills on the Russian River) that the literary-minded Bart left his first poem. First the Wells Fargo and Company treasure box was relieved of $300 and a check from San Francisco's Granger's Bank. But left in its place, on the back of a waybill, was written:

> I've labored long and hard for bred [bread]
> For honor and for riches
> But on my corns too long yove [you've] tred [tread]
> You fine-haired sons of bitches.

Okay, so he couldn't spell. There was also a note to the driver reading, "Driver, give my respects to our old friend, the other driver. I really had a notion to hang my old disguise hat on his weather eye."

The fifth robbery took place on July 25, 1878, and the stage between Quincy and Oroville (in Butte County) was held up for $379, jewelry, and whatever he found in the mail. A second note, unquestionably from the same hand, was found:

> Here I lay me down to Sleep
> To wait the coming morrow
> Perhaps success perhaps defeat
> And everlasting sorrow. Yet come what will, I'll try it once
> My condition can't be worse. And if there's money in that box
> It's munny [money] in my purse.

It was signed "Black Bart—The PO8." The meaning of that "PO8" is still not clear, though we know where he got the Black Bart thing.

By this point, the whole Black Bart business had become very frustrating to both Wells Fargo and law enforcement. According to *It's an Old California Custom*, after

the fifth robbery skilled trackers were hired and followed Bart's trail for sixty miles, but failed to locate him. Eyewitnesses, a mother and daughter, said that a "traveling gentleman" matching Bart's description had stopped by their house. They said his shoes had been cut to make walking in them easier, and he had graying brown hair (getting thin) and deep-set blue eyes. "He looked like a preacher," they said.

Black Bart kept robbing stages regularly through 1883, though he stopped writing poetry for some reason. According to Mary Helmich of California's State Parks Interpretation and Education Division, California Governor William Irwin posted a $300 reward for Black Bart's capture and conviction. Wells Fargo added another $300, and the U.S. Postal Service chipped in $200. James B. Hume, a Wells Fargo investigator, was put on Bart's trail.

A REWARD FOR HIS CAPTURE

In *The Case of Summerfield* by William Henry Rhodes, circa 1871, Black Bart (aka Bartholomew Graham), is described as:

> five feet ten inches and a half in height, thick set, has a mustache sprinkled with gray, grizzled hair, clear blue eyes, walks stooping, and served in the late Civil War under Price and Quantrell (sic), in the Confederate Army. He may be lurking in some of the mining camps, near the foothills, as he was a Washoe teamster during the Comstock excitement.

A $10,000 reward offered by Governor H.G. Nicholson was on his head for the murder of C.P. Gillson, late of Auburn, county of Placer, on the 14th ultimo. Black Bart, the character, was also suspected of robbing the body of the late Gregory Summerfield.

Boles, seen in full regalia as a gentleman. (Wells Fargo)

Wells Fargo investigator James B. Hume helped track Black Bart down—through a laundry mark. (Wikipedia)

CATCHING BLACK BART

Boles/Bart finally came to grief in Calaveras County at Funk Hill. He shouldn't have returned to the scene of his first crime. As the stage approached Funk Hill, Bart did his usual number—he stepped out from behind a rock with his rusty shotgun. Again, as per usual, he asked that the strongbox be thrown down. But this time it was bolted to the floor inside the stage (which carried no passengers at that point). Bart ordered driver Reason McConnell to unhitch the horses while he got to work freeing the box with an ax. Riches were indeed inside: two hundred twenty-eight ounces of amalgamated gold worth an estimated $4,500, $550 in gold coins, and $64 in raw gold.

Meanwhile, McConnell managed to signal to sixteen-year-old Jimmy Rolleri, a passenger who'd temporarily disembarked to go hunting, that he was being held up. Rolleri gave his .44 Henry rifle to McConnell, who fired at Boles—and missed. Apparently the better shot, Rolleri grabbed his gun back and fired, hitting Boles, who as he ran away dropped almost everything he'd taken from the box, plus a bunch of his own things, including a pair of glasses, food, and—fatally—a handkerchief (knotted up and containing buckshot) with a laundry mark.

At the time, such marks were traceable. Hume, along with Detective Henry Nicholson Morse, went to each and every one of the city's ninety-one laundries, and hit pay dirt at Ferguson & Biggs California Laundry. The hankie was easily identified there as belonging to Boles.

Meanwhile, the wounded Boles, exhausted from his work on the strongbox, was able to stash the amalgamated gold that he didn't drop in a rotten log and get away, albeit slowly. It was one hundred miles to Sacramento, but Boles made it, his hand wrapped in another handkerchief. In town, he got a shave and a haircut, went to the tailor for a new suit of clothes, and then caught a train for Reno. He was soon back in San Francisco, with every expectation that he'd gotten clean away.

Unfortunately for him, the Wells Fargo team had been busy, found his boarding house address, and learned he was expected at the laundry. Sure enough, a dandy pulled up at the appointed time, described in Norman Finkelstein's *The Capture of Black Bart: Gentleman Bandit of the Old West* as wearing a "natty little derby hat," with a diamond pin in his lapel, a gold watch in his pocket, and a cane in his hand. "He looked anything but a robber," says Morse in Finkelstein's book. "But I knew I had the man I wanted."

Boles was described as being five feet eight and clean shaven, except for a luxuriant gray moustache. Prison records later said he had heavy eyebrows, a prominent nose, a small mole on his left cheekbone, and was "broad at base."

Under the ruse of wanting to talk to him about mining affairs, the Wells Fargo team escorted Boles to the company's offices where he was grilled. It took a while for him to confess, even though incriminating evidence had been found in his room. Finally, he admitted to having committed the last robbery, and—hoping for leniency—disclosed where the missing gold was hidden. He pled guilty and got six years at San Quentin, which he started to serve on November 21, 1883.

We know that Boles was a gentleman and didn't even smoke or drink. So it's not surprising he was released for good behavior. He worked in the prison hospital as a clerk and asserted that maybe he'd work in a drugstore when he got out. Boles was paroled on January 21, 1888, after serving four years and two months.

HOLLYWOOD'S TAKE ON THE WESTERN

The phrase "throw down that box" was heard from many a Hollywood sound stage. Leonardo DiCaprio's character in *Once Upon a Time in Hollywood* (2019) is a washed-up star in the westerns that had their strongest years in the 1950s. Kids (this author included) often owned both the ten-gallon hat and the cap-gun six-shooters.

It's ironic that Black Bart himself was something of a literary creation. He lived before motion pictures, but one of the very first films to be successful, *The Great Train Robbery* from 1903, is set just two decades after Boles/Bart's crimes. You can watch it anytime, as all twelve minutes are on YouTube. The robbers are quite a bit more bloodthirsty than Bart was.

The western was well established in the silent era. Tom Mix became a big star, as did Hoot Gibson, Johnny Mack Brown, and Ken Maynard.

A milestone of the new talking pictures was *The Virginian* (1929), with Gary Cooper as the good guy Virginian and Walter Huston as the villain, Trampas. That's on YouTube, too, and it introduces us to just about every western movie cliché. A few choice lines are as follows:

"Here's mud in your eye"; "You lowdown buzzard, you"; "I've got you corralled now and I'm calling your hand"; "You want to call me that, smile"; "I got to believe you're a lying, white-livered skunk—this country ain't big enough for the two of us, so I'm giving you until sundown to get out of town—or I'll shoot you on sight"; "Cowhands are dumber than a loco steer"; "You're likely to talk yourself into a heap of trouble"; "She'd look good in an Injun squaw blanket"; "A wild steer is a pretty ornery critter"; "There are some things that are not only loco, they're plumb wrong"; "This country is getting too civilized—I've got a notion that I'm going to be moseying out—to the goldfields or somewhere."

The movie ends up with a classic showdown in the street between cattle rustler Trampas (literally, in a black hat) and the Virginian. Trampas (who of course tries to shoot the Virginian in the back) ends up "dead as a cold mackerel."

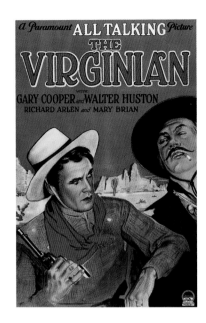

Gary Cooper and Mary Brian in *The Virginian, the early talkie (1929)*
that set up all the western clichés.

Wells Fargo kept tabs on the stagecoach thief after he was out, and Boles felt like a marked man. In February of 1888, he left San Francisco, briefly stayed at the Palace Hotel in Visalia, and disappeared—leaving behind some canned goods, coffee, two neckties, and some shirt cuffs. He was never heard from again. By 1892, Mary Boles (who'd gotten letters from her husband while he was in prison) was listing herself as the widow of Charles E. Boles; at least he was presumed dead.

It's interesting to note that Black Bart was not the only respectable pillar-of-society San Francisco gentleman to steal from Wells Fargo. Charles Wells Banks, British-born like Boles, was the company's top accountant in 1886 when, one day in November, he failed to turn up for work. He wasn't ill; he'd sent his wife east, sold his scientific library, booked passage on the *Star of Papeete* to Australia—and cleaned out the company safe of more than $20,000. The colorful story is told in Alex Gundel's 2019 *Charles Wells Banks' Extraordinary Journey through Life*.

Investigators soon discovered that Banks, like Boles, had been living a double life—and was well known at the city's many brothels. He even ran his own whorehouse, with seven women, quite close to the Wells Fargo office. Banks turned up in the Cook Islands, married (bigamously, one assumes) to the daughter of Queen Matea of Rarotonga. There was no extradition treaty, but the island became a kind of prison—Banks knew if he entered British territory he'd be arrested. He died there in 1915, isolated and destitute, having gone totally blind.

WHERE THEY WENT BAD

With Boles, the turning point was fairly clear. When, at least to his mind, he was cheated out of a mining claim by Wells Fargo and Company, he couldn't just let go and move on to another claim or another profession entirely. The perceived injustice of it ate at him. In his letters, he vowed that steps were going to be taken. And they were, with the added benefit of permitting a luxurious lifestyle without actually having to work. There may have been some principles involved at first, but it appears more than likely that Black Bart just got used to the easy pickings. His callous treatment of his wife and children doesn't say much for his character either.

Black Bart certainly looked the part of the San Francisco gentleman.
(Wikipedia)

WHAT THEY SAID

Boles thought his elegant, upper-class appearance would shield him from suspicion. "Do you take me for a stage robber?" he told his investigators, according to BlackBart.com. "I never harmed anybody in all my life, and this is the first time that my character has ever been called into question."

What follows is the testimony from James E. Rice, former Wells Fargo & Company agent:

> Black Bart was a person of great endurance, a thorough mountaineer who was probably unexcelled in making quick transit over mountains and steep grades. He was comparatively well educated, a general reader, and well informed on current topics. He was cool, self-contained, with humorous tendencies, and after his arrest exhibited genuine wit under most trying circumstances.

JOHN WESLEY HARDIN

(1853-1895)
REVENGE FOR THE WAR OF NORTHERN AGGRESSION

APPALL-O-METER: 9

JOHN WESLEY HARDIN

Hardin claims he was forced into his many killings. (Library of Congress)

THE LEGEND

Making Billy the Kid look like an amateur, Hardin boasted of drilling forty-four men, four of them before he was sixteen. What's more (again, unlike Billy) he lived to be forty-two, wrote an autobiography, and even hung up a shingle as a lawyer. And that was *after* killing those forty-four men. He claimed to have "never killed a man who didn't need killing." A legend was in the making. As Bob Dylan tells it in his fanciful song "John Wesley Harding," he was never known to hurt an honest man, always lent a helping hand, and no charge held against him could be proved. He was never known to make a foolish move. As a friend to the poor, his name resounded across the countryside.

HOW THEY GET IT WRONG

Texan John Wesley Hardin was in actuality a vicious killer and avid racist. If he had redeeming qualities, they're not readily apparent. He was twelve at the end of the Civil War, and his hatred of the freed slaves led him to kill one of them when he was fifteen, inaugurating a life on the run. He might have become a murderer at fourteen, but the classmate he knifed lived to tell about it.

The completion of Hardin's autobiography, *The Life of John Wesley Hardin as Written by Himself*, was interrupted by his murder in 1895. It repeats the notion that he killed only those who needed killing. The preface states, "Hardin, in the latter years of his life, often reiterated that he had never killed a man wantonly or in cold blood, and we believe that this book, evidently written without any purpose of self-justification, will bear him out."

John Wesley Hardin was wanted—and not for taking from the rich and giving to the poor. (Wikipedia)

In reality, the book, published in 1896, was written with a *lot* of self-justification, much of it highly unbelievable. With some of his murders, a fairly tortured scenario was necessary to justify the gunman's self-defense claims. But it worked, because the image of Hardin as an upright fellow who just had to pull a lot of triggers persists.

WHAT WE ACTUALLY KNOW

Hardin was born in Bonham, Texas, in 1853 and had one elder brother, Joe. His father, J.G. Hardin, was a Methodist minister and circuit rider who studied for the bar and was admitted in 1861. His mother, Mary Elizabeth Dixson Hardin, was described by her son as "highly cultured," with "charity predominant in her disposition." The marriage was reportedly harmonious, and the only challenge was that they moved often.

J.G. was an ardent Confederate and organized a company to fight for states' rights, but he was deemed too important at home to go off and fight Yankees. At nine, young John Wesley caught the war fever and was thrashed by his father for planning to run off with a cousin to take up arms.

Like many future murderers, Hardin started with killing animals. However, this doesn't prove anything since decimating the animal population was practically a reflex for many Americans at the time, but it is interesting. "My greatest pleasure was to get out among the big pines and oaks with my gun and the dogs and kill deer, coons, possums or wild cats," he wrote in his autobiography. "If any of those Sumpter boys with whom I used to hunt ever see this history of my life, I ask them to say whether or not our sport in those old days was not splendid."

After moving to Livingston, in Polk County, Texas, the young scholar got into frequent scrapes at school, coming away bleeding, with a scratched face, and black eyes. He claimed it was all in an attempt to live up to his upbringing, trying to be "honest, truthful and brave."

Then things got more serious, with a classmate named Charles Sloter. Hardin claimed young Sloter "wanted to be the boss among the boys" and devised various stratagems to get his rivals out of the way. Sloter claimed Hardin had written some doggerel on the wall about a girl named Sal. Hardin denied it and says that Sloter then came at him with his knife.

"I stabbed him twice almost fatally in the breast and back," Hardin wrote. He was apparently as quick with a knife as he would be later with guns. "A howl at once went up to expel me from the school, some even wanting to hang me. The trustees, however, heard the true facts in the case and instead of expelling me, completely exonerated me and the courts acquitted me." Hardin notes that "poor Charley" was later hung by a mob in an adjoining county.

But he wouldn't be an honest citizen long. The return of the Confederate veterans had evidently left Hardin with a powerful hatred of freed slaves, though it's unclear if his parents' politics further inflamed this. He claimed that Texas at that time was full of "impudent" freed slaves who freely harassed Confederate veterans "and even the weaker sex whenever they had the advantage." In reality, it's hard to imagine how that behavior would not have resulted in a lynching in that place at that time.

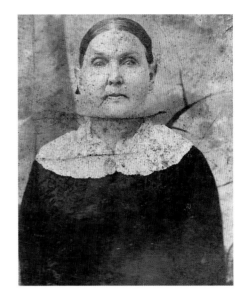

Top: Mary Elizabeth Dixson Hardin was said to be highly cultured—and a die-hard Confederate. (Wikipedia)

Bottom: The young John Wesley Hardin was already getting into serious scrapes. (Wikipedia)

JUSTIFYING MURDER

Hardin was only fifteen when he killed his first man, Mage, not coincidentally a freed slave. To hear him tell it, he was again forced into violence. It began innocently enough with a wrestling match, which Mage lost, getting his face scratched in the process. Being hot tempered, he vowed to kill Hardin and went for his gun. Hardin quotes Mage as saying that "no white boy could draw his blood and live," an attitude that seems hardly likely in immediately postwar Texas.

The pair came across each other the next day on a trail, and Mage is again the instigator and Hardin the peacemaker. Finally, he had to defend himself. "I stopped in the road and he came at me with his big stick," Hardin wrote. "He struck me, and as he did it I pulled out a Colt's .44 six-shooter and told him to get back. By this time he had my horse by the bridle, but I shot him loose. He kept coming back and every time I would shoot again and again until I shot him down….Mage shortly died in November, 1868."

Texas was tough on white people in those days, Hardin claims, and he had to take it on the lam. He states:

> Texas, like other states, was then overrun with carpet-baggers and bureau agents who had the United States army to back them up in their meanness . . . . All the courts were then conducted by bureau agents and renegades, who were the inveterate enemies of the South and administered a code of justice to suit every case that came before them and which invariably ended in gross injustice to Southern people, especially to those who still openly held on to the principles of the South.
>
> To be tried at that time for the killing of a Negro meant certain death at the hands of a court, backed by Northern bayonets; hence my father told me to keep in hiding [until the Northerners were gone]. Thus, unwillingly I became a fugitive, not from justice, be it known, but from the injustice and misrule of the people who had subjugated the South.

Perhaps, surprisingly, this interpretation of the temper of the times carried over into the modern era. "For much of this century, Reconstruction was widely viewed as an era of corruption and misgovernment, supposedly caused by allowing blacks to take part in politics," says *America's Reconstruction: People and Politics after the Civil War.* This interpretation helped to justify the South's system of racial segregation and denying the vote to blacks, which survived into the 1960s.

Far from favoring freed African-Americans, in 1865 the federal government (in the form of Lincoln's successor, Andrew Johnson) issued a proclamation pardoning all Confederates, with the exception of some members of the leadership. Johnson was no supporter of civil rights.

America's Reconstruction states,

> Members of the old Southern elite, including many who had served in the Confederate government and army, returned to power. The new legislatures passed the Black Codes, severely limiting the former slaves' legal rights and economic options so as to force them to return to the plantations as dependent laborers. Some states limited the occupations open to blacks. None allowed any blacks to vote, or provided public funds for their education.

In his version, Hardin took off for his brother's place twenty-five miles distance but was hunted down by some soldiers. They faced off in a creek bed, and when the smoke cleared, two white soldiers were dead and an African-American soldier was lying on the ground, fighting for his life. "I ran up on him and demanded his surrender in the name of the Southern Confederacy. He answered me with a shot." Again, the Colt's .44 spoke its piece—in self-defense, mind you—and by the fall of 1868 there were three more notches in Hardin's gun.

Amazingly enough, Hardin's next move, despite having murdered three soldiers, was to become a schoolteacher. He was liked well enough to get offered another term, he says, but instead had gotten a hankering to be a cowboy, working with his cousins who were cattle drivers. Meanwhile, he also learned to gamble by playing poker, Seven Up,

Portrait of a gunfighter. (Wikipedia)

and Euchre. A betting man, he put money down on horse races, cock and dog fights, and even contests on who could spit the furthest.

Hardin's cousin, Simp Dixon, was just nineteen and a member of the Ku Klux Klan who "was sworn to kill Yankee soldiers as long as he lived." This wouldn't prove to be very long, especially after he hooked up with Hardin—an avowed sympathizer with the man's politics.

With Dixon, Hardin got into a pitched battle in the Richland bottom land with a squad of U.S. soldiers, leaving two of them dead. "Simp killed one and I killed the other, while the rest escaped," Hardin wrote. Soon after, Dixon, "one of the most dangerous men in Texas," was killed by other soldiers in Limestone County.

Sometimes Hardin was accosted in the most innocent of circumstances. "I was young then and loved every pretty girl I met, and at Kosse I met one and we got along famously together," Hardin wrote. But instead of a tale of young love it soon veers off in another direction when a thug threatens to kill him unless $100 is paid. Instead of remuneration, he gets a slug right between the eyes and goes down, "a dead robber." It was still January of 1870, so Hardin had achieved quite a death toll for someone not yet seventeen.

Hardin seemed to be forever getting into situations where men threatened, irrationally, to kill him. A gambler named Bradley was next to fall in this way. After that was a "circus man" who tried to kill Hardin in January of 1870 simply because his arm was brushed while lighting his pipe. Hardin says he apologized politely, but the man would have none of it and went for his gun. Bad move! "He fell with a .45 ball through his head." The next victim, Jim Smolly, was trying to take Hardin in for a reward and was shot, defensively, because he did not have sense enough to throw up his hands at the point of a pistol.

A turkey hunt was interrupted by an Indian shooting an arrow at him, and that fellow ended up dead, too. Card games never ended well. An innocent game of Monte concluded with "a Mexican with his arm broken, another shot through the lungs and another with a very sore head." Five more Mexicans fell victim to his dead aim after they tried to steal cattle from a herd Hardin was guarding. Another gunman got credit for the sixth Mexican.

The young Hardin kills another three men—Davis, Jones, and Smith (the names sounding generic)—when they arrested him and tried to take him to Austin. "Thus I got back my liberty and my pistols," Hardin wrote. "I took an oath right there never to surrender at the muzzle of a gun."

A full recounting of all these murders would get tedious. Fitting some of them into the "I didn't kill anyone who didn't need killing" scenario requires some amazing backflips. The entire Western United States seemed to be conspiring to violently confront him over only the most minor of provocations. The trigger is always pulled when there's no other way to stop the raging bulls.

JOHN WESLEY AND WILD BILL?

Still, there were people who met John Wesley Hardin and lived to tell about it. In June of 1871, Hardin arrived in Abilene, Kansas, whose reputation had made an impression. "The town was filled with sporting men and women, gamblers, cowboys, desperadoes and the like," Hardin wrote. "It was well supplied with barrooms, hotels, barber shops and gambling houses, and everything was open. Before I got to Abilene, I had heard much talk of Wild Bill [Hickok], who was then marshal of Abilene. He had a reputation as a killer." Of course, Hardin had the same reputation, so they were bound to meet.

Tom Clavin's *Wild Bill: The True Story of the American Frontier's First Gunfighter*, describes their meeting. "When he arrived in Abilene, Hardin had no particular plans other than to see what all the fuss was about in this particular Kansas cow town," Clavin wrote. "He knew who Wild Bill Hickok was, but it was possible that at least at first the marshal did not know Hardin. Or he didn't care all that much, if the only outstanding warrant on him was from Texas, and Hickok was not all that fond of the state."

Hickok reportedly told Hardin that the town had a no-gun ordinance and asked for the killer's shooting irons. In Hardin's account, he got the better of Wild Bill by employing the "road agent's spin"—seeming to hand the weaponry over, but then rapidly reversing them and pointing the muzzles at the famous mustachioed marshal.

Clavin doubts that Hickok would have fallen for this old trick, but in any case, nobody ended up dead in that encounter. Hardin's dialogue for Hickok is laughable. "You are the gamest and quickest boy I ever saw," Hickok supposedly said. "Let us compromise [on] this matter and I will be your friend. Let us go in here and take a drink, as I want to talk to you and give you some advice."

"Hickok made Hardin a deal—the marshal would pretend he had no knowledge of the Texas warrant if the teenager refrained from killing anyone while in Abilene," Clavin wrote. Of course, since everyone in the world was trying to kill Hardin for no good

*Despite his many killings, Hardin was "rehabilitated" in jail, studied the law, and
actually practiced as an attorney. (Wikipedia)*

reason, that pact couldn't last. In fact, that very night a robber snuck into Hardin's room at the American Hotel and got a bullet for his troubles. Hardin, although blameless, had broken the pact and was again on the run—stealing a horse and leaving in such a hurry his pants stayed behind.

Hardin went back to Texas, where (after using the same trick that supposedly worked on Wild Bill Hickok) he killed one African-American lawman who was trying to arrest him and wounded another. He claimed that the state, now run by Republican Governor E. J. Davis, was in the control of "carpetbaggers [and] scalawags from the North, with ignorant negroes frequently on the force." He declared war on "negro or Yankee mob rule and misrule in general." He vowed not to rest until "it is a thing of the past for a negro to hold an office." Hardin seems to have forgotten that the Civil War was over, and the South had lost.

Did Texas under Davis (1869 to 1873) fit Hardin's picture? In some cases, yes. African-American police officers were sworn in. And the state did become a haven for carpetbaggers, and there was copious corruption and voter fraud. But Davis also championed law and order, and he strengthened the school system. J.W. Hardin represented a challenge to any government that didn't condone wholesale killing of its citizens and elected representatives.

The killings continued. In September of 1871, Hardin says "a posse of negroes from Austin" came after him. "I met them prepared and killed three of them," Hardin claimed. "They returned sadder and wiser." Soon after this Hardin married his sweetheart, Jane Bowen, in Gonzales, Texas. The newlyweds would not have been surprised to have had the wedding invaded by police, but Hardin says they would have been met with "a warm reception."

In July of 1872, Hardin was gambling with a fellow named Phil Sublet, a sore loser who couldn't handle being taken for $35. He went and got his gun and shot Hardin, with a pair of buckshot going in near his navel. Hardin was starting to recover but was wounded again—twice—when posses came to arrest him. Finally jailed, he escaped with the aid of sympathetic citizenry and returned to his "darling and beloved wife" in Gonzales, Texas, staying peacefully with her and recuperating until January of 1873.

Back on the road with his cattle drives early that year, Hardin killed the apparently insane J. B. Morgan, who wanted to share a bottle of champagne with the outlaw but went berserk with bloodlust when his offer was declined. Oddly enough, Hardin did eventually face justice for this casual murder, by his account being indicted for it four years later. He pled guilty to a charge of manslaughter and served two years for his crime.

The law was beginning to close in on Hardin, but there were still bullets in his gun. On May 27, 1874, he was accosted by Charles Webb, deputy sheriff of Brown County, and shot the man dead. In Hardin's self-serving telling of the story, Webb had proclaimed that he held no ill will toward the young outlaw, but then proceeded to try and shoot him in the back. Hardin was wounded in the left side during the incident. Shooting Webb would also catch up with him.

OTHER JOHN WESLEY HARDING

American singer-songwriters can't get enough of John Wesley Hardin for some reason. In addition to Bob Dylan's song and album, there is also John Wesley Harding, the pen name for Wesley Stace. He's English, and also a novelist. Under the Harding name he's made seventeen albums and toured with Bruce Springsteen (not Dylan, though; that would have been interesting). His novels, which have won multiple awards, are under his real name, as is his most recent album. He's currently teaching at Swarthmore.

I wrote to ask Harding/Stace why we romanticize outlaws, and why he took that name, but I'm still waiting for a reply. He did explain his choice to the *New York Times*, stating that it was all about the Dylan album and the fact that both Hardin and he were descended from John Wesley, the founder of Methodism. He calls Hardin a "cowboy," which is a stretch, and adds that of the two, he's followed Wesley's teachings more carefully and also "killed fewer people." Let's hope so!

Wesley Stace, aka John Wesley Harding. (Wikipedia)

CAUGHT IN FLORIDA

With a $4,000 bounty on his head, Hardin fled to Gainesville, Florida, where he opened a saloon, killing six more men in the process. In Florida, Hardin joined a mob that burned a black man to death for allegedly assaulting a white woman. The coroner, who'd been among the mob the night before, declared that the man had accidentally burned himself to death.

In July of 1877, after a terrific struggle, John Wesley Hardin—proclaiming himself the most innocent man who ever lived—was finally taken into custody in Pensacola, Florida, by a force led by Texas Rangers Lieutenant John B. Armstrong and including Escambia County Sheriff William H. Hutchinson and nine Escambia County deputies. They caught Hardin as he was attempting to board a train at the old L&N Freight Depot. The location is in what is now downtown Pensacola. In arresting him, Hardin was told, "John Wesley Hardin, you are the worst man in the country, but we have got you at last." And they did have him. He was tried for the Webb shooting and other crimes and was given twenty-five years in prison the next year. Of course, it was a travesty of justice, Hardin says.

Hardin never misses a chance to proclaim himself a victim of circumstances, and he loved putting the exoneration in other people's mouths. On the way to jail, he met a man who'd come all the way from Memphis to meet him. The fellow proclaims, "Why, there is nothing bad in your face. Your life has been misrepresented to me. Here is $50. Take it from a sympathizer."

Did Hardin rehabilitate himself in jail? Improbably, after trying repeatedly to escape, he became an avid reader, studied theology, and became superintendent of the Sunday school, president of the debating society, and a law student. The unfinished manuscript of Hardin's autobiography ends abruptly as he is obtaining the books that will enable him to pass the bar.

In reality, Hardin did pass the bar after he was released in 1894. His beloved wife, Jane, had died in the interim. Hardin remarried to Callie Lewis in 1895, but it didn't

Opposite: Lawman John Henry Selman, who gunned Hardin down— but was shot himself the very next year. (Wikipedia)

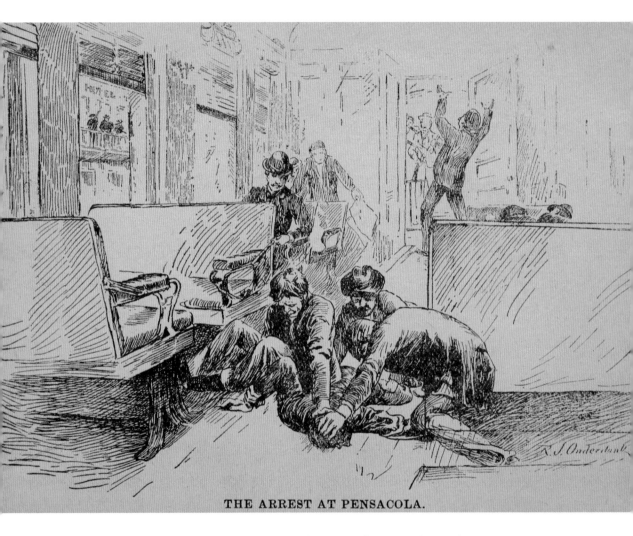

THE ARREST AT PENSACOLA.

John Wesley Hardin taken into custody—finally—in Florida. (Everett Collection Inc./Alamy Stock)

last long. He moved to El Paso, hung up his legal shingle, and began writing the autobiography. The book was incomplete because Hardin had started threatening John Selman, whose son had arrested Hardin's then-girlfriend, Beluah M'rose, for vagrancy and for displaying a gun in public. Some accounts say that Hardin had pistol-whipped Selman. On August 19, 1895, Selman gunned Hardin down as he was throwing dice at the Acme Saloon Bar in El Paso. The manuscript was published posthumously in 1896. Selman was acquitted, but also died violently, also after gambling, in 1896.

It's interesting to note that if Hardin had held on a few more years, he would have found himself in a very different world, one with automobiles and airplanes, and very few saloon/gambling dens populated by armed men with horses tied up outside.

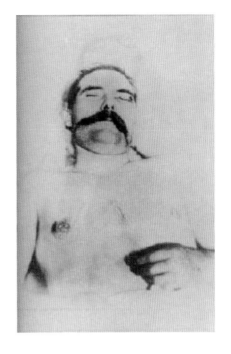

The wages of sin. John Wesley Hardin, postmortem. (Wikipedia)

WHERE THEY WENT BAD

Well, where Hardin went bad is clear enough. Young scholars don't usually stab their classmates nearly to death. Hardin wasn't destined for the straight life, which is a shame because he appears to have been of above-average intelligence—smart enough to work as a teacher and pass the bar after studying law books in prison. But from a very young age, Hardin was a one-man wrecking crew. It's unclear how many people he actually killed. History.com says the toll "might have been as high as 40." It seems fair to assume that at least some of the dead didn't deserve their fate.

WHAT THEY SAID

Hardin on school (from his autobiography):

> I always tried to excel in my studies, and generally stood at the head. Being playful by nature, I was generally first on the playground at recess and noon. Marbles, roily hole, cat, bull pen and town ball were our principal games and I was considered by my schoolmates an expert. I knew how to knock the middle man, throw a hot ball and ply the bat.

Hardin on life during Reconstruction (from his autobiography):

> In those times if there was anything that could rouse my passion it was seeing impudent negroes, lately freed, insult or abuse old, wounded Confederates who were decrepit, weak or old. There were lots of those kind in the country in the 1860s, and these negroes bullied both them and even the weaker sex whenever they had the advantage. Frequently I involved myself in almost inexplicable difficulties in this way.

Hardin on snoring (from History.com): "They tell a lot of lies about me. They say I killed six or seven men for snoring. Well, it ain't true. I only killed one man for snoring."

ISOM DART

(1849-1900)

RODEOS AND STOCK THEFT

APPALL-O-METER: 3

ISOM DART

THE LEGEND

What legend? It's safe to assume that most readers of this book haven't heard of the man. The name Isom Dart is not up there with Jesse James, Billy the Kid, and John Wesley Hardin, and in part that's because all the legendary bad men of stage, screen, and pulp fiction were white. Of course, notoriety is not exactly desirable, but it's fame of a sort. And African-American cowboys and lawmen—of whom there were many—were also erased from history.

HOW THEY GET IT WRONG

In popular entertainment, and in some popular history, too, the West has been homogenized. White Anglo-Saxons not only rule, they make up the whole population. Even the few Mexicans are mostly there for comic relief. In more recent revisionist Westerns, with *Deadwood* being a prime example, the notion of a polyglot frontier is at least suggested.

By 1825, *Smithsonian* recounts, "Slaves accounted for nearly 25 percent of the Texas settler population. By 1860, 15 years after it became part of the Union, that number had risen to over 30 percent—that year's census reported 182,566 slaves living in Texas." These are the same African-Americans, freed after the Civil War, who were found so objectionable by John Wesley Hardin. Returning ranchers recruited these skilled workers as cowhands, so African-Americans herding cattle was a common sight on the frontier.

The genealogy site Geni.com estimates that twenty

Left: George Fletcher, born in 1890, was an African-American cowboy who came over the old Oregon Trail from Missouri. He was a ranch cowboy until he died in 1973. (CowboysofColor.org)

Opposite: Ned Huddleston, aka Isom Dart. He was a skilled cowpoke. (Wikipedia)

An eighteenth century Mexican cowboy. (Wikipedia)

percent of all cowhands were African-American. The term "buckaroo" may in fact be derived from the African word "bakara," meaning "white man, master, boss." This is not to suggest that all was equal on the frontier. William Loren Katz' *The Black West: A Documentary and Pictorial History of the African-American Role in the Westward Expansion of the United States*, recounts that "discrimination did exist on the trail and at the ranch." Many African-Americans were hired to do the hardest work around the outfit, Katz recounts. "When subjected to hazing, African-American cowmen relied on a tactful restraint rather than retaliatory fists and six guns," he writes. An exception was John B. Hayes, known as the "Texas Kid" (see page 78).

And most of the skills associated with cowboys today came from Mexican vaqueros (literally "cow men"). As *National Geographic* reports, "Two decades before the pilgrims landed in 1620 on Plymouth Rock . . . adventurous *criollos* (Spanish-born Americans) and *mestizos* (mixed Spanish and Indian settlers) pushed past the Rio Grande River to take advantage of land grants in the kingdom of New Mexico, which included most of the western states."

They'd been herding cattle in the Americas since 1598, which was the year Don Juan de Oñate sent an expedition with 7,000 head across the Rio Grande into present-day New Mexico. One out of every three cowboys in the late 1800s was the Mexican *vaquero*, says Kendall Nelson, a photographer and author of the book *Gathering Remnants: A Tribute to the Working Cowboys*.

WHAT WE ACTUALLY KNOW

Isom's real name was Ned, but he changed it when this very competent cowboy became an outlaw. He was born an Arkansas slave in 1849, and his owner was a Confederate officer who took him to Texas during the Civil War. He may have acquired his thieving ways during that conflict, when as a camp attendant and cook he was sent out by his Confederate masters to forage for cattle, chickens, and anything else edible.

Freed in 1865, and taking the last name Huddleston, he headed for the Texas-Mexico border region where he was hired at a rodeo. Huddleston's skills with a horse were in demand. Riding, roping, and busting broncos, the six-foot two-inch man, acquired the nicknames "Black Fox" and the "Calico Cowboy."

Huddleston began to diversify into criminality, and he and a young Mexican bandit named Terresa rustled horses in Mexico and sold them in Texas. He came up to Wyoming and Colorado around 1871 as part of a cattle drive to Browns Park. He had some success mining gold and silver but claimed he got cheated by his partner.

Huddleston also hooked up with a Chinese gambler, with whom he had disagreements, and was briefly jailed under suspicion of having murdered the man. He was held in jail with the man he'd accused of cheating him out of mining profits, and they had a violent confrontation. But Huddleston—still mostly on the right side of the law—was released when the Chinese partner turned up alive and well.

The Tip Gault Gang, accomplished cattle rustlers. (Wikipedia)

THE STRAIGHT LIFE?

Attempting to go straight, Huddleston worked construction and found work as a bronco buster. *Black People Who Made the Old West*, by William Loren Katz, quotes a contemporary "Westerner" as saying, "I have seen all the great riders, but for all-around skill as a cowman Isom Dart was unexcelled . . . . He could outride any of them, but he never entered a contest." Another added, "No man understood horses better."

What apparently turned the benign Huddleston into the notorious Isom Dart was a failed love affair with a Shoshone Indian woman in 1875. It left him

CIVIL RIGHTS PIONEERS

Not much is known about John "The Texas Kid" Hayes, but the African-American cowboy was reportedly a champion rider from Waco, Texas. His signature was to look for "whites-only" saloons, which he would enter and ask for a drink. If he was refused, Hayes would return on his horse, ride through the door, and shoot out all the lights before leaving town.

A fellow traveler—at six foot four inches and 245 pounds—was Jess "Flip" Crumbly of Cheyenne, Wyoming. He reportedly got his nickname because anyone he punched would flip backwards at great speed. He was said to have taken his drinks wherever he wanted.

bitter, and that same year he returned to Browns Park and the criminal life. He joined the infamous Tip Gault Gang, whose membership included Jack Leath, Joe Pease, and Terresa, Dart's old rustling companion. They rustled horses and cattle out of southeastern Wyoming. A ranch Dart established in Browns Park, around 1890, was suspected of having been built from stolen stock.

Despite his thieving ways, Dart was universally known to be a gentle fellow and never violent. When one of his fellow rustlers was injured during a raid, Dart agreed to stay behind and nurse him. "For a day and a night he stayed with his dying companion, and then dug his grave," Katz recounts.

Unbeknownst to Dart, while many of his neighbors considered him a stand-up fellow, the ranchers whose cattle he may have rustled had other ideas. The entire Gault Gang was ambushed, with Dart the only survivor.

According to John Jarvie in the *Browns Park BLM Cultural Resources Series,*

> All of the gang were killed except Huddleston who jumped into the grave
> and played dead. Ned eventually crawled out of the grave and stole a horse
> from a nearby ranch to make his getaway. The rancher spotted him and
> managed to shoot him in the leg as he rode away. Exhausted from the loss
> of blood, Ned fell off of his horse and passed out on the trail. Miraculously,
> Ned was discovered and nursed back to health by William 'Billy Buck'
> Tittsworth who, as a youngster in Arkansas, had lived on a plantation
> neighboring Ned's. The two men had been close friends in their youth
> and had not seen each other for years before that fateful night on the trail.
> Huddleston managed to get to Green River City where he caught the first
> train out of town.

Bass Reeves was a man of high integrity, and on the right side of the law. He brought in his own son. (Wikipedia)

The law came in more than one color. Bass Reeves is in the first row at left, with cane. (Wikipedia)

BLACK MAN WITH A BADGE

Racism made it easier for people of color to become outlaws than to become lawmen in the Wild West, though Bass Reeves—born a slave in 1839 Arkansas—surmounted numerous barriers to become a deputy U.S. Marshal, working under the federal "hanging judge" Isaac Parker.

Bass, who escaped to neutral ground in Indian Territory during the Civil War, was formally freed in 1865 with passage of the 13th Amendment and returned to Arkansas, where he married and eventually became father to eleven children. Because he was so familiar with the ways of the Seminole and Creek tribes (and even learning their languages after a fashion), Reeves was recruited in 1875 by U.S. Marshal James Fagan to work under Judge Parker—the first African-American deputy west of the Mississippi. The six-foot two-inch Bass was to hold jobs as a federal lawman in the region for more than thirty years.

Reeves said he'd arrested more than 3,000 felons in his long careers, and killed fourteen outlaws. He was handy with both rifles and pistols and was a master of disguise. He arrested white, African-American, and Native American people if they got on the wrong side of the law. Reeves once even arrested one of his own sons, Bennie Reeves, for the murder of his wife. When Bass heard a deputy talking about giving the case to someone else, History.com quotes him as saying, "Give me the writ."

At the end of his life, with Oklahoma a state at last, Reeves became an officer in the Muskogee Police Department, serving for two years. One of Reeves' descendants was Paul L. Brady, the first African-American appointed as a federal administrative law judge (in 1972).

Reeves life story is told in the 2006 book *Black Gun, Silver Star: The Life and Legend of Frontier Marshal Bass Reeves* by Art Burton. The author claims that Reeves may have been the inspiration for The Lone Ranger, based on some casual evidence. "He is the closest person in real life to compare to the fictional hero," Burton said in a 2007 interview.

Reeves knew Belle Starr and probably Cherokee Bill, whose gang was arrested and hanged by Judge Parker.

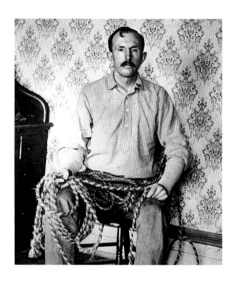

Tom Horn is credited with taking out the fearsome outlaw Isom Dart. (Wikipedia)

A FATAL ENCOUNTER WITH TOM HORN

One version of events has it that Dart had hooked up with local rangers Matt Rash, Jim McKnight, and Annie "Queen Ann" Bassett (an intimate of Butch Cassidy) to steal cattle from the stock king Ora Haley. Tom Horn, the famous Pinkerton detective, was hired—maybe by Haley but also perhaps by ranchers John Coble, Coble's partner, Frank Bosler, and likely the giant Swan Land and Cattle Company—to take Dart out of the picture permanently. Rash was found murdered in his cabin in July of 1900, having tried to write the name of his killer in his own blood. Dart must have known he was a marked man but refused to leave Browns Park. Horn and his Winchester allegedly ambushed Dart at his cabin there on October 3, 1900. The kind-hearted rustler, who befriended and babysat his neighbors' children, was fifty-one.

A *Washington Post* book review speculates that Dart may have been killed by Butch Cassidy, but in fact it was another legend feted in Hollywood. According to an account published by the Wyoming State Historical Society:

> In 1900, many historians have concluded, Horn murdered two suspected cattle thieves, Matt Rash and Isom Dart, in Browns Park, where the Colorado, Utah and Wyoming borders intersect. A foreman for the ranchers who hired Horn was quite firm, in an account written down 20 years later, that Horn had done the crimes. The crimes received little notice in Wyoming.

Local opinion was mixed, with some thinking that Dart had gone back to the straight life. He was a likable fellow. According to Katz' account in *Black People Who Made the Old West*, at one point Dart was arrested by a deputy sheriff on castle-rusting charges, but on the way back to face justice, the buckboard crashed and the sheriff was knocked unconscious. Instead of taking the opportunity to flee, Dart tended to the man's wounds then drove him to the hospital. After that, he turned himself in. At the trial it was decided that anyone who could act in such a manner must be innocent, and Dart was acquitted. "He rode back to Browns Park a new man," Katz wrote.

Horn wrote his own story in *Life of Tom Horn: Government Scout and Interpreter*, but the shooting of Isom Dart didn't get a mention. He tended to portray his life working for the cattle barons as chiefly that of a stock detective, rounding up stray herds.

Horn, portrayed in the movies by Steve McQueen as a former gunslinger working for the real-life cattleman John Coble, was never prosecuted for the murders of Dart or Rash. But he was hanged in 1903 for the shooting of fourteen-year-old Willie Nickell, a crime depicted in the *Tom Horn* film. Horn allegedly confessed to that killing, with a rifle from 300 yards, calling it "the best shot that [he] ever made and the dirtiest trick that [he] ever done." Other accounts say he was innocent, the confession coerced, and the trial rigged. That's how the movie tells it.

AFRICAN-AMERICAN COWBOY NAT LOVE MEETS BILLIE (SIC) THE KID

Not many African-American cowboys wrote memoirs, but Nat Love—the real deal, as well as a former slave like Dart—is the author of *The Life and Adventures of Nat Love Better Known in the Cattle Country as Deadwood Dick by Himself*, published in 1907. According to scholar William Loren Katz, it's the only full-length autobiography by an African-American cowhand.

There's no doubt that Love was an accomplished cowboy and could throw a rope, ride a bucking bronc, and herd cattle with the best of them. He also liked a good whopper. "Deadwood Dick" was a literary creation of dime novelist Edward Lytton Wheeler, and Love is one of many to claim to have inspired the character.

The most amusing story in his book is a completely imaginary encounter with Billy the Kid that has him, Zelig-like, present at the key moments. Keep in mind that young Henry McCarty, as he was known then, was born in New York City of Irish-American parentage. His racist views would have likely made friendship with an African-American on equal terms unlikely.

"The first time I met Billie (sic) the Kid was in [Anton Chico], New Mexico, in a saloon, when he asked me to drink with him, that was in 1877," Love wrote. "[The Kid] was hired by John Chisholm to rustle cattle for him. Chisholm agreed to pay the Kid so much per head for all the cattle the Kid rustled."

Chisholm and the Kid fell out over payments and, according to Love, the Kid would then kill anyone working for Chisholm on the spot. Love said:

> And few men were quicker with a .45 or a deadly shot than 'Billie the Kid.' The next time I met the Kid was in Holbrook, Arizona, just after a big round up….The 'Kid' showed me the little log cabin where he said he was born. I went in the cabin with him, and he showed me how it was arranged when he lived there, showing me where the bed sat and the stove and table. He then pointed out the old post office, which he said he had been in lots of times. He told me he was born and raised in Silver City, New Mexico . . .

> The Kid bid me good bye. He said he was going to the mountains as he knew them well, and once there he was all right, as he could stand off a regiment of soldiers. The three of them departed together. I never saw him again until the spring of 1881. I was in the city of [El Morro, New Mexico], and saw him the morning he was forced to flee to the mountains to escape arrest. We could see him up there behind the rocks. He was well armed having with him two Winchesters and two .45 Colts revolvers and plenty of ammunition, and although the officers wanted him badly, no one dared go up after him as it was certain death to come with range of the Kid's guns . . .

Well, it makes a good story. And the Kid did invent origin stories for himself that had him born far from New York City. Love spent his later years living in Los Angeles where he worked as a guard at a securities company. He lived until 1921, undoubtedly lamenting the passing of the frontier.

Nat Love had a fascinating history, but he loved tall tales, too—and told one about befriending Billy the Kid. (Wikipedia)

WHERE THEY WENT BAD

It was love that done it, some say. He became embittered by his love affair with an Indian woman in 1875. But the actual roots probably go back further to when young Ned was still a slave. He was inculcated by his Confederate masters into the idea that he could take what he needed; cattle included. It was an idea to which he would repeatedly return.

WHAT THEY SAID

"In my 51 years, I've seen the evil that men do. For their nature is to prey on each other. The toils of man do burden the soul and I was about to unveil a dark heart." Dart didn't leave an autobiography, as so many of these men did in surprisingly literate times. Did he actually say this near the end of his life, or is it a product of the writer's pen? It's unclear, but it sounds fake.

The quote is to be found at the end of a discussion about an eponymous screenplay that was written about Dart, described as "the *Dances with Wolves* for the African-American male." Dart in this telling was "a hard man who lived in harder times, a flawed hero branded an outlaw" who "eventually found his way to peace and glory." The fictional Dart gets the drop on Tom Horn, spares his life, but is then shot in the back by the cowardly Horn with two blasts from the aforementioned Winchester.

PEARL HART

(BORN 1871, POSSIBLY DIED 1955)

CELEBRITY STAGE ROBBER

APPALL-O-METER: 3

PEARL HART

THE LEGEND

The smirking Pearl Hart has been called "Arizona's most notorious famous bandit."
Dressed in men's clothes, she would boldly hold up stagecoaches, with her male
companions following her direction. And she even wrote poetry to glorify her deeds.
Here's some of her verse, from an untitled poem that was published in the *Yuma Sun*
some years after her crime:

> The sun was shining brightly
> On a pleasant afternoon.
> My partner speaking lightly said the stage would be here soon.
> We saw it coming around the bend and called on them to halt.
> Then to their pockets we did attend.
> If they got hurt 'twas their own fault.

"The foul-mouthed, cigar-smoking desperado" Pearl Hart "became notorious as a
bandit queen and jail breaker," according to Marina Michaelides' *Renegade Women
of Canada*. "She didn't steal much cash, but she stole the public's imagination with
romantic tales of woe." She was a protofeminist, who famously told the court that since
women had no hand in writing the law, they shouldn't be held to account by it. And in
case you missed it, she was notorious.

HOW THEY GET IT WRONG

Pearl Hart's legend is based on only *one* botched stagecoach robbery, which just
happened to be the last of its kind. She and her hapless accomplice got away with
the loot but left a trail a blind man could follow. She was no master criminal, just a
woman—raised with every possible advantage—who'd rather make her money the easy
way and then live as wildly as possible until the moolah was gone.

*Pearl Hart posed for these armed photos after she
was arrested. The press couldn't get enough of her.
(Arizona Historical Society)*

WHAT WE ACTUALLY KNOW

The woman who would become Pearl Hart was born Pearl Taylor in Lindsay, Ontario, in 1878. She grew up in a comfortable, middle-class family. Friends described her as a lively, outgoing teenager who liked to date.

An acquaintance from that period is effusive, telling the Arizona Historical Society:

> She was a pretty girl and had a wonderful figure and voice; could imitate a croaking frog, an owl, a hawk, could sing like a mockingbird . . . was lithesome, blithe and witty; gushing with fun and jollity; also a wonderful dancer, and very attractive. Everybody admired her and was proud of her acquaintance; but she possessed one detrimental fault which brought her many troubles. She was too amorous; accepted too many dates with handsome young men, which finally caused her undoing.

That's pretty accurate. The accomplished young woman had a decidedly wild side. She was said to have grown up reading about the eighteenth century British highwayman Richard "Dick" Turpin and his faithful mare, Black Bess. Instead of Black Bart's "throw down that box," Turpin exclaimed, "Stand and deliver." The tall tales led young Pearl Taylor to run away on several occasions, sometimes taking her younger sister along on adventures.

When she was just sixteen, Taylor ran away for good with a man named Frederick (some say Frank or William) Hart, who gave her his name and not much else. A worthless layabout who refused to work (except to earn money for liquor), he got her pregnant and physically abused her. In 1893, the pair traveled to the Columbian Exposition in Chicago where Fred worked sporadically as a sideshow barker and Pearl found odd jobs (and reportedly saw sharpshooter Annie Oakley perform).

Pearl left and reconciled with Fred several times, and by him had two children who ended up with her mother, who had moved to Ohio. But finally, Taylor had had enough. She left Hart and headed south across the border. The newly minted Pearl Hart was free to follow her dark childhood dreams.

Hart later told *Cosmopolitan* magazine, "I was only 22 years old. I was good-looking, desperate, discouraged, and ready for anything that might come. I do not care to dwell on this period of my life. It is sufficient to say that I went from one city to another until sometime later I arrived in Phoenix, Arizona."

A stagecoach robbery in progress. By 1899, the stage had almost passed into history. (Wikipedia)

ROBBIN' THE STAGE

The stage, as it were, was being set. In Phoenix, Hart took up with another worthless character: a dance hall musician and "tin horn gambler" named Dan Bandman, who reportedly taught her how to drink, smoke, and use opium. The best thing Bandman did for her was to disappear by enlisting in the Spanish-American War. Hart got some work cooking for miners in Mammoth, Arizona, but it was too much like work.

In Globe, Arizona, she finally met her partner in crime, the German-born Joe Boot. He won her affection by driving former paramour Bandman off when he showed up looking for money.

"On top of all my other troubles," Hart later recalled to *Cosmopolitan*:

> I got a letter just at this time saying my mother was dying and asking me to come home if I wanted to see her alive again. That letter drove me crazy. No matter what I had been, my mother had been my dearest, truest friend, and I longed, to see her again before she died. I had no money. I could get no money. From what I know now, I believe I became temporarily insane.

Since every legitimate venture (including mining) that Boot and Hart tried had failed, it was time to do a Dick Turpin. "Stand and deliver!"

According to the *Copper Area News*:

> On that infamous day [May 30, 1899], Henry Bacon was sitting atop the stagecoach as the driver. He had a Colt .45 revolver on him but it was not loaded as he did not expect to use it. The days of Indian raids and stagecoach robberies were presumably long gone. In fact, the Florence to Globe line was one of the few stagecoaches which had not yet been replaced by the railroad.

There were three passengers, one Chinese, one a traveling salesman, and the third a "tenderfoot."

Boot and Hart were, like Black Bart before them, on foot. As Bacon slowed to take a sharp turn at Cane Springs, the bandits, unmasked, sprang out from their hiding places. Hart wore men's clothes, but the disguise was far from perfect.

The take wasn't bad. Hart, in a jailhouse interview with *Cosmopolitan* magazine that appeared in October 1899, said, "Joe told me to search the passengers for money. I did so, and found on the fellow who was shaking the worst [the salesman] $390."

The tenderfoot had $36 and the Chinese passenger had $5. Hart and Boot got it all, plus the salesman's watch. The victims were in consensus that Hart was the brains of the operation, with Boot following her orders, though she said otherwise in her interviews.

Not quite as genteel as Black Bart, Hart and Boot nonetheless made some chivalrous gestures.

"The stage-driver had a few dollars," Hart said, "but after a council of war we decided not to rob him. Then we gave each of the others a charitable contribution of a dollar apiece and ordered them to move on, Joe warning them all not to look back as they valued their lives."

This was the high point of Pearl Hart's criminal career. They robbed the stage and got away with the loot. It was downhill after that. Pinal County Sheriff W. E. Truman couldn't miss the trail the novice fugitives left, and caught up with them at a schoolhouse twenty miles south of Benson. The desperadoes were sleeping it off. "We were awakened by yelling and shooting [and] found we were looking straight into the mouths of two gaping Winchesters in the hands of the sheriff's posse," Hart told *Cosmopolitan*.

According to Globe-based *Silver Belt* newspaper, the officers confiscated the weaponry with no problems. When woken, Hart went right for her guns. According to the *Belt*, she "sprang up, fighting, but the man made no resistance." Boot, a real sad sack, was described by the *New York Times'* contemporary account as "paralyzed with fright." All the money was recovered.

Top: Pearl Hart striking a pose in jail. (Wikipedia)

Bottom: Pearl and her six guns. One hopes they weren't loaded. (Wikipedia)

Hart reading her fan mail. She became despondent when the public eye moved elsewhere. (Wikipedia)

A STAR IN JAIL

A female bandit was a novelty, so Hart was much attended and photographed by the press. She was shipped to the Pima County jail in Tucson because they could better accommodate the attention. Even the new *Cosmopolitan* magazine sought and obtained an interview. "I was easily impressed," she told the magazine.

Again, from the *Belt*: "The camera fiends have taken shots of her with all sorts of firearms and looking as much the desperado as they can make her." We can see the results today. It's kind of amazing that her jailers let a prisoner pose with firearms, but that indeed happened. She even kept a pet wildcat, or at least posed with one. Hart is smirking in all the shots—she was proud of herself, a childhood fantasy fulfilled.

The *Silver Belt* of July 27, 1899, reports that Hart had become somewhat despondent when the media stopped fussing over her. She had to be closely watched so she could not secrete enough morphine to kill herself. "She has already attempted to remove herself from mundane affairs by means of an overdose of the drug," it said. Morphine in jail? Apparently yes, in 1899.

Ironically, the reporters listened to Hart's tale of robbing the stage to get the money to visit her dying Canadian mother and proclaimed it a fake. "The Canada tale is a fake," the paper said. "The woman is from Toledo, Ohio, where her parents, well-to-do people, still reside." But, of course, she really *was* Canadian. Hart's mother had only recently moved to Ohio.

Hart was pretty good at bending men to her will, and she seduced a trusty named Ed Hogan, who cut a hole in the wall of her cell. According to Ed Butts' *She Dared: True Stories of Heroines, Scoundrels, and Renegades*, Hogan promised to organize a new outlaw gang, and Hart would be its queen. She couldn't resist that proposition. With her new lover, Hart escaped, leaving behind a note proclaiming support for female suffrage.

The pair made it to Deming, New Mexico, where they were recognized from the *Cosmopolitan* story and were captured. Ed Hogan was a trusty no more. Hart and Boot were tried on June 15, 1899. Although Hart had freely admitted her involvement to the press, at her trial she pled not guilty and, amazingly enough, was acquitted.

Judge F.M. Dean didn't accept the verdict, had Hart rearrested, and chided the jury for dereliction. This second time, she was charged with stealing the coach driver's pistol,

Pearl Hart's pistol on display at the Yuma Territorial Prison. (Wikipedia/Marine 69-71)

Hart displays her characteristic defiant smirk. (Wikipedia)

was convicted, and got five years. Boot was also convicted with a thirty-year sentence, but after he was made a trusty, he escaped, in 1901, and was never heard from again.

Transferred to Yuma, Hart evidently puffed on cigarettes the whole trip and entertained a posse of guards with her antics.

As an inmate serving her sentence at the Yuma Territorial Prison (one of just twenty-nine women who had stayed there at the government's insistence), Hart led a charmed life, enjoyed a large cell, and continued to pose for the press with shooting irons. At the end of 1902, she was pardoned by Territorial Governor Alexander Brodie. According to *American Cowboy* magazine, "The pardon came with the stipulation that Pearl Hart would leave the territory and never return. With it, came speculation that Pearl was once again with child and a risk to Brodie's and the prison's public perceptions."

Not much is known for certain about Hart's life after prison. She was said to have taken part in a vaudeville show about her life, with the money coming from that well-known stage door Johnny, William Randolph Hearst. Another version has her going to New Mexico and briefly starring in a play, "Arizona Bandit," written by her sister. Other reports place her with Buffalo Bill's Wild West show, but though Bill loved such spectacles, it seems unlikely. It was even claimed that she later revisited the jail (which closed in 1909 and is now a national park) and took the tour.

The only definitive sighting comes from 1904 when Hart, then running a cigar store in Kansas City, was arrested and charged with receiving stolen goods. She was acquitted. Speculation places her in New York or San Francisco, but a stronger theory is that the amorous bandit married a local Pinal County rancher and lived peacefully outside Globe, not far from the Cane Springs site of the stage robbery. If so, she broke the terms of her pardon. That woman died in 1955 (denying she was Pearl Hart). If she was indeed that historical figure, the pistol-packin' momma made it to eighty-four years old.

WHERE THEY WENT BAD

Pearl romanticized bandits. It's too bad her head got filled early on with swashbuckling tales of highwaymen. Judging from her future associates—nearly all men of bad repute—she never got over those youthful fantasies.

Sally Scull's grave marker. She was camera shy in life.

HORSE THIEF AND HUSBAND KILLER?

Sarah Jane Newman, also known as Sally Scull (or Skull), was suspected of being both these things in her short, eventful life. She was born into an Illinois family in 1817, but moved to Texas in 1823, joining Stephen F. Austin as a member of the Old Three Hundred original Anglo settlers.

Young Sarah/Sally grew up in the Texas Territory at a time when Indian attacks were frequent—her mother, Rachel, reportedly stopped one Comanche invader by cutting off his toes when his foot came through the door. She also stopped one coming down the chimney by throwing a burning pillow into the fireplace.

According to historian Bartee Haile, writing in the Texas-based *Plainview Herald*, Sally showed early moxie, indicating a willingness to take on hostile Indians when full-grown adults quailed. She married her first husband, Jesse Robinson, an Indian fighter, at age sixteen in 1833. The day they got married, he and his volunteer parties drove off a war party.

Robinson fought in the Texas Revolution and received a land grant near Gonzales. The marriage produced two children but didn't last—both parties wanted a divorce (Sally was suspected of adultery with a hired man known only as "Brown"), and Robinson got custody of the children. Sally promptly married again, but gunsmith George Scull (or Skull) didn't live long—he was dead by 1849. "Rumors of foul play [on Sally's part] still abound," writes *True West* in the 2002 article "Wild Women of Texas." Sarah kept his surname, though.

A third husband, John Doyle, got hitched to her in 1852, but he too soon succumbed, "with Doyle either drowning during a river crossing or by his wife's lethal hand," Haile wrote. Scull was known to be an excellent shot, and according to the book *Texas Bad Girls*, a Texas Ranger, John S. Ford, claimed he heard a shot, saw a man falling, and a woman in the act of lowering a six-shooter.

> She was a noted character named Sally Scull. She was famed as a rough fighter, and prudent men did not willingly provoke her in a row. It was understood that she was justifiable in what she did on this occasion, having acted in "self-defense."

There was a fourth husband, Isaiah Wadkins, who the *Handbook of Texas* says lived to talk about it, but in other sources she either drowned him (in a barrel of whiskey) or shot him in the head.

Sally was a crack shot, knife handler, and an adept horse trader (probably also a horse thief). She ran illegal cotton across the border with Mexico during the Civil War (which resulted in a blockade of Texas ports).

A European traveler, Julius Froebel, wrote an admiring description of Sally in his journal, *Seven Years' Travel in Central America, Northern Mexico, and the Far West of the United States*, published in 1859. He described her as follows:

> a North American Amazon, a perfect female desperado, who from inclination has chosen for her residence the wild border-country on the Rio Grande. She can handle a revolver and bowie-knife like the most reckless and skillful man; she appears at dances (fandangos) thus armed, and has even shot several men at merry-makings. She carries on the trade of a cattle-dealer, and common carrier. She drives wild horses from the prairie to market, and takes her oxen-waggon, along through the ill-reputed country between Corpus Christi and the Rio Grande.

Believe it or not, Sally got married a fifth time, this time to an unredeemed low-life named Chris Horsdorf (nicknamed "Horse Trough"). It's not clear what happened to Horse Trough, or to Sally herself, because after a sighting in Goliad, Texas (where she was acquitted of perjury in 1866) she disappeared from history. Perhaps she was murdered for her money (she had a lot) by her villainous husband, or maybe she murdered him and then (having exhausted the local supply of willing husbands) moved on to new and more fertile matrimonial territory.

WHAT THEY SAID

A protofeminist, Hart, in addition to standing up for women's suffrage, allegedly proclaimed at her trial, "I shall not be tried under a law in which my sex had no voice in making."

Hart told *Cosmopolitan* that the stagecoach robbing was Boot's idea. "'Joe,' I said, 'if you will promise me that no one will be hurt, I will go with you.' 'A bold front,' he said, 'is all that is necessary to rob any [stagecoach].'" Well, it's true that no one got hurt. And the bold front worked for Black Bart.

On her enduring love for Joe Boot, Hart said, again in the *Cosmopolitan* interview:

> His entire trouble was brought on by trying to get money for me to reach mother. We took an oath at parting never to serve out a term in the penitentiary, but rather to find that rest a tired soul seeks. It is, of course, public that I tried to kill myself the day they separated me from Joe at Florence and today I am sorry I didn't succeed.

This is an apparent reference to an overdose of morphine, but was Hart—the toast of Yuma Territorial Prison—really all that desperate? She served only two years.

CHEROKEE BILL

(1876-1896)

A KILLING SPREE

APPALL-O-METER: 9

CHEROKEE BILL

Cherokee Bill was an enigma, though his love for his mother is not in dispute. (Wikipedia)

THE LEGEND

Like Billy the Kid, Cherokee Bill died young and left a good-looking corpse. The name will sound vaguely familiar, and it's one you're likely to associate with chuck wagons, roundups, and cheery cowboy songs around a crackling fire. "Oh, look over yonder, here comes 'ol Cherokee Bill!" But he was in no way that kind of person.

HOW THEY GET IT WRONG

As with Isom Dart, there's not much of a written record about Cherokee Bill. With racism prevailing, in the publishing industry as well as elsewhere, men and women of color didn't attract much notice in the popular press or the dime novels. And he lived a very short life, without really explaining his bloody crime spree. Was he racially motivated, embittered by a society where racism was ingrained, and people of mixed descent were treated especially badly? He declined an opportunity to make that claim, and it's negated by the fact that his very first shooting victim was African-American.

WHAT WE ACTUALLY KNOW

Born Crawford Goldsby in 1876 at Fort Honcho, Texas, Cherokee Bill terrorized the Indian Territory before being hanged—at age twenty—in 1896. He was of mixed race—African-American, Sioux, and Caucasian from his father, George Goldsby (a former buffalo soldier); and Cherokee, African-American, and Caucasian from his mother, Ellen Beck.

His early years were spent mainly living apart from his parents, a circumstance that might have fueled some of his later bitterness. When he finally did reunite with his mother, she had remarried (in 1889) and was working as a laundress for the army while living at Fort Gibson, in Indian Territory.

Young Crawford did not get along with his stepfather, William Lynch. Other caregivers report finding him difficult, too. According to the 1994 report, "The Toughest of Them All," by Bennie J. McRae, Jr. posted at the African-American history site Lest We Forget at Hampton University, "He began to associate with unsavory characters, drink liquor and rebel against authority."

Perhaps trying to get Crawford away from his bad companions, when he was fifteen, he was sent away to live with his sister, Georgia, and her husband, Joseph "Mose" Brown, near Nowata, Oklahoma Territory. Mose, too, found Crawford hard to take, so the stay was short. Returning to Fort Gibson, he stayed with some distant relatives. More trouble was brewing, but first there was a short period of calm.

At seventeen, Crawford was employed by performing odd jobs, cleaning stores, and working on ranches. In one of the few positive reports about Crawford Goldsby, McRae writes that he was described by a ranch owner named James Turley as a "quiet, good-natured, hard-working boy, well-liked by all who knew him." We know the last part of that isn't true—he was intensely disliked by some of his own relatives.

Cherokee Bill during his brief reign. (Wikipedia)

A SHORT-FUSED HOT HEAD

He may have worked hard, when he worked, but chronic hotheadedness would have made it difficult for him to maintain steady employment. Murder sort of gets in the way of that, too. At eighteen, in 1893, he attended a harvest dance at Fort Gibson with the intention of seeing and tripping the light fantastic with pretty fifteen-year-old Maggie Glass.

That was innocent enough, but things went awry when he confronted thirty-five-year-old Jake Lewis, an African-American who had a dispute with Goldsby's younger brother. Unfortunately, Lewis easily overpowered Goldsby, and this left the younger man embarrassed in front of his would-be girlfriend. "Being a good loser was not in Cherokee Bill's makeup," says an account, "Cherokee Bill," at DarkCanyon.net.

Brandishing a six-shooter, Goldsby threatened to shoot Lewis, and a couple days later made good on the claim, gunning the older man down on his farm with two shots. Lewis eventually recovered and filed charges, so Crawford Goldsby was now a fugitive from justice. Shortly after, he went into tribal lands and hooked up with brother criminals Jim and Bill Cook, also mixed-race, part-Cherokees.

In June of 1894 a posse of lawmen led by Sheriff Ellis Rattling Gourd tracked down Goldsby—by now calling himself Cherokee Bill—and the Cooks to Tahlequah, Oklahoma, and the subsequent shootout at Fourteen Mile Creek left deputy lawman Sequoyah Houston dead on the ground and Jim Cook injured.

From here on, Cherokee Bill (blamed for the fatal shot) was a wanted murderer, and he handled the matter by doubling down and going on a bloody crime spree with the Cook brothers and other unsavory characters. Their names reportedly included Texas Jack, Sam McWilliams (aka "The Verdigris Kid"), Skeeter Baldwin, and Chicken Lucas.

Cherokee Bill became, as *Explore Magazine*'s "Badass of the Month" article on him proclaimed, a "down-and-dirty, shoot-first plague on humanity without a single redeeming quality besides his unstoppable desire to murder, pillage, rob and destroy everything he could get his hands on." The gang was integrated; does that count as a redeeming quality?

Around this time, all of Cherokee Bill's hair fell out, reportedly an ancestral issue inherited from his grandfather. This can't have improved his disposition. A chronology of his subsequent crimes are as follows:

July 4, 1894 The gang celebrated Independence Day by shooting Kansas and Arkansas railroad man Samuel Collins (who'd been trying to eject a drunken companion of Cherokee Bill's) through the bowels. A derelict who happened to be on the scene was also shot. Both men died. Bill was fingered.

July 6, 1894 Another railway man, a station agent named A.L. "Dick" Richards, was also shot dead. Bill took credit, then later denied the crime.

July 18, 1894 The gang robbed the Wells Fargo Express Company and the St. Louis and San Francisco railroad train at Red Fork.

July 30, 1894 Another robbery, this time the Lincoln County Bank in Chandler, Oklahoma. They got $500. J.B. Mitchell, who happened to be on the scene, got a fatal bullet.

September 1894 Cherokee Bill, who got in trouble in the first place for defending his brother, sent mixed signals about family, by murdering his brother-in-law, the same Mose Brown who had earlier taken him in and showed prescience by taking an instant dislike to Bill, young as he was then. The disagreement was variously said to be over some swine, or the family inheritance.

October 1894 This was a busy month for the gang. They robbed the Katy express office at Chouteau, Oklahoma, pillaged the Missouri Pacific depot at Claremore, and the same railroad's Kansas City and Memphis Express at Corretta.

November 8, 1894 Cherokee Bill and Sam McWilliams went to Lenapah in Indian Territory to rob the Schufeldt and Son store. They ordered the owner to open the safe, and while he was complying, a crowd gathered outside the store's window. For no apparent reason, Cherokee Bill fired through the window, pointlessly killing a curious onlooker named Ernest Melton.

A CHARMER?

Despite him being a mad-dog killer, McRae reports that Cherokee Bill "had an irresistible charm with women," and supposedly had a girlfriend in every section of the territory. His dalliances contributed to his downfall, as similar escapades did in the youthful Billy the Kid.

It's interesting to note that the gang didn't hit a very wide area, staying close to familiar territory. You'd think they wouldn't be that hard to track down, but local lawmen had a perhaps understandable desire not to end up dead—Bill was a sharpshooter. Later, more mobile gangs—led, for instance, by John Dillinger (who loved his Ford V8s)—took in a much wider territory.

Union agent Dew Wisdom contacted the Bureau of Indian Affairs in Washington to ask for help, stating that the region was being terrorized and that local law enforcement wasn't up to the task of hunting down Cherokee Bill, whose killings (many of them unprovoked) totaled between seven and thirteen. The dragnet closed in with help from Deputy U.S. Marshal W.C. Smith. Most of the gang was caught or killed.

Cherokee Bill was finally brought to justice using what used to be referred to as a "honey trap." Bill was still sweet on Maggie Glass, who, like him, had mixed Cherokee and African-American heritage. An informant told the lawmen about Bill's visits to a cabin near Nowata, and when he showed up, the law was waiting for him.

Ike Rogers, who owned the cabin, plied Bill with whiskey laced with morphine, and then he hit the bandit over the head as Bill leaned into the fireplace to light a hand-rolled cigarette. The blow would have killed a lot of other people, but it just made Bill mad, and there was a big struggle. Eventually, the outlaw was subdued and cuffed.

On the way to justice at Fort Smith, Arkansas, Bill proved his reputation true by snaking out of the handcuffs, but the lawmen managed to bring him to heel. In his jail cell, he plotted escape. With a Colt revolver smuggled into him, he managed to shoot

Judge Isaac Parker made short work of Cherokee Bill. (Wikipedia)

guard Lawrence Keating in the stomach then again in the back. But Bill was met with jail reinforcements and surrendered without further gunplay. Since sentiments against Cherokee Bill were running high and there was doubtless a shortage on character witnesses, a date with the hangman was set.

On April 13, 1895, the celebrated hanging judge, Isaac Parker, scheduled September 1895 for Bill's execution. According to the *Handbook of Texas*, the judge called the outlaw "a bloodthirsty mad dog who killed for the love of killing." When Bill's mother started crying hysterically in the courtroom, the laconic Cherokee Bill responded, according to the *Explore* article, "Hey, I ain't dead yet." The fatal day was delayed to March 17, 1896. And then a three-hour stay was arranged so the doomed man could meet with his family.

A year later, Clarence Goldsby—Bill's brother, previously believed to be peaceful— gunned down Ike Rogers, the man who slipped Cherokee Bill a mickey. "The first ball took effect on Rogers' body," a contemporary Kansas City newspaper account said on April 22, 1897. An African-American bystander was wounded. The Goldsbys stood up for each other; they were a tight-knit family.

Judge Isaac Parker's courtroom, where Cherokee Bill received his sentence, recreated at Fort Smith. (Wikipedia)

Juliet Galonska reports that the number thirteen was apparently unlucky for Crawford Goldsby. After he killed Ernest Melton, the reward for his capture was $1,300. His death sentence was proclaimed on April 13, and Judge Parker took thirteen minutes to charge the jury in the killing of Larry Keating. The trial took thirteen hours, with thirteen witnesses for the prosecution. The jury took thirteen minutes to find him guilty, and he died at 2:13 p.m.

THE LAST DAYS OF CHEROKEE BILL

Juliet Galonska wrote about the last days of Cherokee Bill for the National Park Service. She says he appeared unconcerned about what was to happen to him and spent his dwindling time playing poker with other prisoners. With five days left, though, he met with Father Pius of the German Catholic Church and continued to meet with him every day thereafter.

On St. Patrick's Day, Bill woke up early and was heard singing and whistling. His family visited later that day. Meanwhile, 2,000 to 3,000 spectators had gathered around the gallows. The scene "though not disorderly, was one of indescribable excitement," a local paper of the time said. People perched on an old shed, which collapsed.

The death warrant was read, and Father Pius intoned a prayer. At noon, a black hood was put over Cherokee Bill's head and his arms tied. At 12:13 p.m. the trap door opened and he fell six feet, breaking his neck. He was buried at Fort Gibson, and is there today.

Cherokee Bill meets his maker, in an artist's conception. He was there to die, not make a speech. (Courtesy of Special Collections, University of Arkansas Libraries, Fayetteville)

WHERE THEY WENT BAD

Young Crawford Goldsby may have gone bad anyway, but there's no doubt still-fresh memories of the horrific Trail of Tears weighed on him, as did the lack of opportunity and pervasive racism he found on the frontier. He appears to have become not a rebel with a mission but a nihilist and misogynist who loved only his mother.

WHAT THEY SAID

Cherokee Bill was eloquent on the gallows. Asked for last words, he said, according to *Explore*, it was "about as good a day to die as any." Asked if he had any other final words, Bill issued this undying quote, "I came here to die, not make a speech," adding, "Goodbye, all you chums down that way." When he saw his mother in the crowd, he said, according to Jerry Akins' *Hangin' Times in Fort Smith: A History of Executions in Judge Parker's Court*, "Mother, you ought not to have come up here." She replied, "I can go wherever you go." Akin also has Bill saying, "Proceed with the killing business."

JESSE JAMES

(1847-1882)

REFIGHTING THE CIVIL WAR

APPALL-O-METER: 10

JESSE JAMES

THE LEGEND

Jesse James gets off easy. He's remembered not for his bank and train robberies but for getting shot in the head as he was hanging a picture. The biopic, directed by Andrew Dominik and starring Brad Pitt in the title role, is called *The Assassination of Jesse James by the Coward Robert Ford*.

Okay, maybe he didn't deserve to get waylaid that way, but does his sad end justify a seeming canonization? Ron Hansen, who wrote the book on which that movie is based, told the *Seattle Times* in a 2007 article entitled "A Story of Myth, Fame, Jesse James," "When I was starting to write the book, one of my colleagues said that the 19th century has really been influenced by two James families: William and Henry James in the East, and Frank and Jesse James in the West. They shaped American consciousness."

In Dominik's movie, the traitorous Bob Ford (Casey Affleck) says to Jesse (Pitt) that, many a night, he stayed up reading about the bandit's escapades. "They're all lies, you know," Jesse replies. Indeed, most of the positive stuff was lies, but the robberies and murders were certainly real.

Jesse (top) and Frank James (bottom). They rode together, as Confederates and as criminals. (Minnesota Historical Society)

HOW THEY GET IT WRONG

Since he's up there with Billy the Kid as one of America's most famous outlaws, we tend to want him to be a more sympathetic character than he actually was. Brad Pitt plays him as positively soulful. However, the truth was different. In answer to Hansen, let me state it clearly: Jesse James was a murderous cheap crook with no redeeming factors. The only thing he "shaped" was the untimely conclusion to the lives of anyone (particularly African-Americans) who got in his way. And maybe a few movie Westerns.

The Missouri State Historical Society sums it up in a "Historic Missourians" portrait, pointing out that Jesse James:

Jesse James left a romantic legacy he didn't deserve. (Wikipedia)

> became a legend in his own lifetime by committing crimes supposedly out of revenge for the poor treatment he, his family, and other Southern sympathizers received from Union soldiers during the Civil War. James sought personal recognition and publicity by writing letters to the press. His crimes terrorized innocent civilians and stifled economic growth in Missouri in the years following the Civil War.

It's interesting that James' defense is exactly the same as the one presented by John Wesley Hardin in his posthumously published autobiography.

This stance may have been popular in the South, but it aligns James firmly with the Ku Klux Klan and other Confederate sympathizers who didn't like the outcome of the conflict. In James' case, his passions played out by brutal acts on the Kansas-Missouri border in the war's wake. He killed at least a dozen people, and possibly seventeen. How this benefited the poor is unclear. They didn't get any of the money, despite what that song says.

DISTORTING HISTORY

It requires contortions to turn figures like Jesse James into heroes, but those contortions were most definitely made in the post-war South. Here's an aggrandizement of these people by Major John N. Edwards in his 1877 book called *Noted Guerrillas: Warfare of the Border*, which is a passionate defense of, among others, the murderous Confederate raider William Clarke Quantrill.

> It required, indeed, all the excesses of the Civil War of 1861-1865 to produce the genuine American guerrilla—more enterprising by far, more deadly, more capable of immense physical endurance, more fitted by nature for deeds of reckless hardihood, and given over to less of penitence or pleading when face to face with the final end, than any French or Spanish, Italian or Mexican guerrilla notorious in song or story. He simply lived the life that was in him, and took the worst or best as it came and as fate decreed it.
>
> Circumstances made him unsparing, and not any predisposition in race or rearing. Fought first with fire, he fought back with the torch; and branded as an outlaw first in despite of all reason, he made of the infamous badge a birthright and boasted of it as a blood-red inheritance while flaunting it in the face of a civilization which denounced the criminals while condoning the crimes that made them such.

It's a short distance from this background to Edwards' loving portrait of the bandit Jesse James. James' son's 1899 biography, *Jesse James, My Father: The First and Only True Story of His Adventures Ever Written*, reads:

> The blue eyes—very clear and penetrating—were never at rest. His form— tall and finely molded—was capable of great effort and great endurance. On his lips there was always a smile, and for every comrade a pleasant word or a compliment. Looking at the small, white hands with their long, tapering fingers, it was not then written or recorded that they were to become with a revolver among the quickest and deadliest hands in the West. Jesse's face was something of an oval. He laughed at many things. He was light-hearted, reckless, devil-may-care. He was undaunted.

WHAT WE ACTUALLY KNOW

Jesse Woodson James (his real name) was born in Clay County, Missouri, in 1847, the third of four children of Kentuckians Robert and Zerelda Cole James. They married in 1841, when Robert was twenty-three and Zerelda sixteen. Robert James, who studied at Georgetown College, was a Baptist minister. He was also a farmer, with a 225-acre property, and a slave owner. He abandoned the family to preach to the gold miners in California and never came home, dying in a gold mining camp in 1850. Before he died, according to a 2019 *National Geographic* account, "Jesse James: Rise of an American Outlaw," he sent his wife a letter asking her to "kiss Jesse for me" and to "ask God to help you to train your children in the path of duty."

Opposite: Jesse James' .44-caliber Hopkins & Allen pistol was an 1873 model. (Library of Congress)

Right: The James homestead in Kearney, Missouri, during the 1880s, a sketch from a photograph. (State Historical Society of Missouri)

According to the *National Geographic* portrait, "Slavery was everywhere in western Missouri, with its numerous tobacco and hemp farms. Clay County counted 2,742 slaves in 1850, and six of them belonged to Reverend James." A young slave was actually sold to finance Robert James' ill-fated California trip.

The Kansas-Missouri border area was a stage set for conflict over slavery. The Kansas Territory had to decide (based on the Kansas-Nebraska Act of 1854) whether to join the Union or the Confederacy, and it was influenced both by proslavery advocates and abolitionists (including John Brown) who pushed the territory in the other direction. Bloody battles ensued for four years, with more than fifty people killed on both sides.

Jesse James, in white hat, with Frank, seated, and Charles Fletcher Taylor at left, taken in 1864. (State Historical Society of Missouri)

At the outbreak of the Civil War in 1861, Jesse James, Jr. wrote in his biography of his father, "The feeling in those days was very intense against Southern sympathizers. Northern spies in Southern uniforms would go to families and get a drink of water or something to eat, and the families would be persecuted for it and sometimes put in jail."

It didn't take long for the violence to engulf the James family, which had joined Governor Clairborne Fox Jackson in supporting the Confederacy. Frank James, Jesse's eighteen-year-old, Shakespeare-loving brother, went off to join the Confederates, but was quickly captured and sent home. He swore a loyalty oath to the Union but soon was off again to join Quantrill's Raiders, attacking abolitionists, Union troops, and even civilians who showed sympathy for the federals.

The James farm was raided by Northern militiamen in 1863, and again Jesse's son takes up the story. Wanting to know the whereabouts of Quantrill, Jesse, Jr. asserts that the soldiers beat his stepfather, Dr. Reuben Samuel, almost to death. Jesse, then sixteen, was also savagely beaten. When the brutality proved unavailing, the soldiers "pointed their guns at my grandmother, and said, 'You had better tell what you know.'"

Jesse's mother, a die-hard Confederate, reportedly refused to cooperate, whereupon the soldiers said they were going to kill Dr. Samuel and "let the hogs eat him." While that did not happen, in the raid's aftermath Jesse's course was set. "I will join Quantrill," he said, according to Jesse, Jr. There were some in the community who thought that Jesse James would become a minister, as he was religiously devoted, but now his path lay before him. "After that day, Jesse was out for blood," *National Geographic* quotes Frank James saying years later.

Top: Frank James set an example—a bad one—for his brother. (State Historical Society of Missouri)

Bottom: William "Bloody Bill" Anderson put the James brothers to work, marauding and killing, including at the infamous Centralia Massacre. (Wikipedia)

JESSE, OUT FOR BLOOD

Both Frank and Jesse James soon signed up with a Quantrill splinter group led by William "Bloody Bill" Anderson and saw considerable action. Jesse was wounded in the chest during a summer 1864 guerrilla raid. In September of that year, Frank James (and quite likely Jesse) joined Anderson in an infamous raid on Centralia, Missouri, that became known as the Centralia Massacre.

First, the raiders (numbering between 350 and 400) sacked Centralia itself. What follows is from an 1882 *History of Boone County* by newspaper publisher William F. Switzler.

> The stores of Ball and Sneed were robbed of nearly every article they contained. Goods were taken for which the bushwhackers had no use—calicoes, muslins, women's shoes, even baby slippers. The robbery was wanton and indiscriminate. The depot also was plundered….There was also a barrel. 'What's in this? By golly! It's whisky!' In five seconds the head was broken in and 'anti-prohibition' flowed down the throats of the guerrillas like water after a long and sultry ride.

Next, a train was raided; $3,000 taken from its safe, and twenty-two unarmed Union soldiers—on leave from General William Tecumseh Sherman and traveling home—were systematically stripped, murdered, mutilated, and scalped. Again, from the *History*:

Probably 25 men opened on the doomed line [of Union soldiers] with revolvers at 20 paces. Expert pistol shots as they were, many of the guerrillas missed their aim. A dozen of the prisoners, shot through the brain or the heart, fell dead at the first volley. Others screamed and staggered about with hands pressed to their wounds until, shot again, they tumbled lifeless to the ground.

After that, 123 of 147 Union soldiers under the command of Major A.V.E. Johnson (most armed only with pistols) were killed with muzzle-loading Enfield rifles. Only three raiders were killed and ten wounded. No quarter was given. According to the *History*, Union Captain Smith caught a guerrilla's horse by the bridle and declared, "I always spare prisoners." The guerrilla responded with, "I never do" and shot the captain dead. It was one of the most merciless scenes of carnage in the entire Civil War. Again, there was stripping, mutilating, and scalping of the dead soldiers.

Many accounts claim that Jesse James was present at the Centralia Massacre and personally killed Major Johnson, but the *History* calls these tales "silly"—it says the

From Harper's Weekly, *"The destruction of the city of Lawrence, Kansas, and the massacre of its inhabitants by the Rebel guerrillas, August 21, 1863." (Library of Congress)*

future bandit leader was lying wounded at that time in Carroll or Chariton counties. Frank James "was at Centralia, and took a full hand," the report said.

National Geographic, however, did place Jesse James at the scene of the Centralia Massacre. "Jesse, on a fleet horse at the head of the charge, galloped to within a few feet of the Union commander and knocked him out of his saddle with a pistol shot to the head," the magazine said. Many other reports, including one from PBS, claim a teenage James was present. Regardless if he was there or not, Jesse's sympathies were certainly with the raiders.

Ted Yeatman's *Frank and Jesse James* reports that both brothers were indeed on the scene. "Major Johnson was reportedly shot down in the onslaught by Jesse James, at least according to brother Frank," Yeatman wrote. But he also quotes guerrilla Jim Cummins, who said he "heard of several parties having boasted of killing Major Johnson," and that it was "very difficult to know in such a general mix-up who did the killing."

"Bloody Bill" would not live long, because the full fury of the Union Army was visited on his head, and only a month after Centralia, he was ambushed near Albany in Ray County. Bill and a number of his troop were killed, with the bushwhacker's body hung up on display at the courthouse.

KILLING UNARMED MEN

An Army scout named Sam Cox headed the party that took out "Bloody Bill." According to PBS, "The murder of unarmed men became of hallmark of Jesse James' life of crime, and the motive for the 1869 Gallatin bank robbery, the first that Jesse was known to have committed, was James' desire to kill Samuel Cox and thereby avenge Bloody Bill's death."

With the war all but lost, on May 15, 1865, Jesse James (still a bushwhacker) was shot through the right lung during a battle with a Federal patrol. James' family claimed he was on his way to surrender. James was nursed back to health by his cousin, Zerelda "Zee" Mimms, later his wife (they married in 1874) and mother to his four children (including Jesse, Jr.).

One of the most famous pictures of the swashbuckling Jesse James. (Library of Congress)

Now James was set on revenge, and killing Samuel Cox was high on his to-do list. The Missouri State Historical Society says in its "Historic Missourians" account that James' career as a criminal may have begun as early as 1866, when the Clay County Savings Bank was robbed (during daylight hours, a first) of $60,000 (an enormous sum at the time) and an innocent bystander was wounded (or killed). According to some accounts, Jesse did not take part but Frank James likely did, along with comrade in arms Cole Younger. Two years later, in 1868, "Jesse and Frank James took part in robbing a bank in Kentucky," the historical society wrote.

The James Gang was forming at the same time Missouri was changing. Not only was slavery now prohibited, but becoming a citizen, holding office, or teaching school required taking the "Ironclad Oath" denying any Confederate activity or sympathies.

The honorable Captain John W. Sheets, murdered in a case of mistaken identity during a bank robbery by Jesse James. (Wikipedia)

A NEW LIFE OF CRIME

The first robbery that Jesse James positively *was* involved in took place at Gallatin, Missouri, a county seat of less than 1,000 people, on December 7, 1869, and the Daviess County Savings Association was the target. The bandits got $700. A lawyer was wounded, and the cashier was senselessly shot dead. Jesse James apparently believed it was Sam Cox they'd killed.

The dead man's name was actually Captain John W. Sheets, "an honorable man" who was "held in high esteem by the citizens of Daviess County and the town of Gallatin," reported the *Gallatin North Missourian* in 1993. Sheets' military title referred to his service in the Civil War on the Union side. At the time of his murder, he was a civic-minded citizen and the former two-term sheriff of Daviess

Jesse James smites his many enemies. (Everett Collection Inc./Alamy Stock Photo)

FRANK JAMES.

From Photograph taken in March, 1882, and presented to author of "Border Outlaws."

Frank James, from a photograph, March 1882. (Everett Collection Historical/ Alamy Stock Photo)

The murder of Captain Sheets, seen in a contemporary illustration. (Daviess County Historical Society/Wikipedia)

County, with previous six years of service as a circuit clerk, four years as county recorder, and was also a former county commissioner.

A horse abandoned by the fleeing bandits was identified as Kate, owned by Jesse James. "The citizens of Gallatin were positive that the two men who shot Captain Sheets were the James boys and a reward of $3,000 for their capture was posted," the *North Missourian* reports. Some $500 of the reward money was posted by Mary Sheets, the dead man's wife. "There is a boldness and recklessness about this robbery and murder that is almost beyond belief," wrote the *Kansas City Daily Journal*.

One Daniel Smoote filed a civil case asking Frank and Jesse James to pay $223.50 to replace a horse, saddle, and bridle the brothers stole when fleeing the bank. They failed to appear in court, so Smoote won his judgment (but never collected). More serious charges were coming.

Frank and Jesse James were indicted for murder, and Jesse (by then twenty-two) responded to this by writing the governor to claim he'd been elsewhere, with his alibi backed by "some of the best men of Missouri." He also said in a letter that was published during June of 1870 in the *Liberty Tribune*, that he would be willing to surrender to the state's civil authorities, but, given the danger of being caught and hanged by out-of-control lynch mobs, would "never surrender myself to be mobbed by a set of bloodthirsty poltroons." He claimed to have lived as a "peaceable citizen" since the Civil War.

John Newman Edwards, editor of the Kansas City Times *and a former Confederate officer. The idea of the James boys as Robin Hoods traces to him. (State Historical Society of Missouri)*

It turns out he didn't have to surrender. The editor of the *Kansas City Times*, John Newman Edwards, was a former Confederate major and he took up the James boys' cause, claiming they were at home during the bank robbery. He also laid it on thick about the brothers' glorious record of defending the South in the Civil War.

Jesse was "wantonly and unjustly hunted and denounced by all who have partisan passions to gratify," the *Times* fatuously puffed. Edwards was also likely the main source of the Jesse-James-as-Robin-Hood myth. "Edwards' objective was to restore a sense of pride in the defeated Rebels, and Jesse James proved the perfect symbol for him," says *Bill O'Reilly's Legends and Lies: The Real West*.

Amazingly enough, it worked, and the governor issued a statement absolving the brothers of involvement in the robbery. They were never forced to account for murdering Sheets or robbing the bank. That undoubtedly emboldened them to continue their life of crime. Now united with Cole Younger and his brothers (John, Jim, and Bob)—all of them former Confederate guerrillas—the bank and stage robberies continued, in Iowa, Texas, Kansas, and West Virginia. Train robberies were added in 1873.

In the summer of 1871, the James-Younger gang hit a bank in Croydon, Iowa, as most of the good citizens were attending a speech in the Methodist Church by orator Henry Clay Dean. Again, the James Gang was needlessly violent, murdering the unarmed cashier. After stealing $6,000, they rode over to the church and waved the stolen money at the assembled crowd.

The James Gang was still seeing sympathy in print. In 1872, a *Kansas City Times* headline proclaimed: "A Card from Jesse James. He Denies All Complicity with the

Exposition Robbery." As late as August 1876 the *Times* was still claiming Frank and Jesse were innocent men. "Whenever a train robbery or a bank cracking operation transpires in any portion of the United States, the James and Younger boys receive all the censure," the paper reported. "They are the first names mentioned, and all the blame, all of the criminality, is centered upon them. The majority of the people living in this section of the country do not believe that Jesse and Frank James or the Younger boys are guilty of all the great robberies charged against them during the past few years."

The villains, in this telling, were the "unsophisticated St. Louis and Chicago detectives" trying to make a name for themselves.

Cole Younger survived to write a book about his exploits. (Library of Congress)

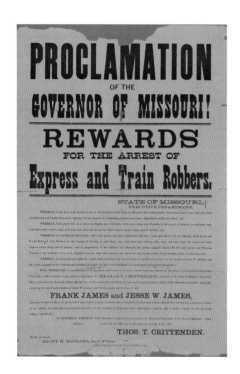

A ROBBERY GOES WRONG

In September 1876, a raid on a bank in Northfield, Minnesota, went seriously wrong. The brothers' Confederate politics were once again part of the decision to rob that particular location. First National Bank was, according to a PBS American Experience account, where former Mississippi Governor Adelbert Ames (also a former Union general) kept his money.

According to Bryce Stenzel in the *Mankato Free Press*:

> The primary reason [they raided Northfield] had much to do with settling old scores left over from the Civil War, a decade earlier. It should be remembered that both the James and Youngers had all been Southern guerilla fighters from western Missouri [and] held the entire Union responsible (and especially the military leadership of the North) for their families' personal suffering, as well as that of their friends.

Jesse led two other robbers into the bank, while five more stood on guard outside. Told by the bookkeeper that the vault was on a time lock and couldn't be opened, the three held a Bowie knife to the man's throat and cracked him over the head with the butt of a pistol. Instead of a fortune, the gang scored bags of nickels worth $23. By this point the local citizenry had heard the commotion and began gathering outside with guns. Most of the gang was killed (Charlie Pitts) or captured (the Younger brothers), with only Frank and Jesse escaping—not before they shot the blameless bookkeeper dead.

Both Frank and Jesse were wounded in the encounter, Frank in the right leg and Jesse in the thigh. All three Youngers were captured. Cole lived through a long prison sentence and, after being released, was an occasional business partner of Frank James. In his self-serving autobiography, *The Story of Cole Younger, by Himself*, published in 1903, Younger claims that he had urged that nobody be harmed in the robbing of the bank, and that neither he nor the James brothers were the inside men. Younger's book echoes Newman in claiming that Southern patriots such as himself were forced into a life of crime via the "War of Northern Aggression."

It's a good thing the robbery failed. According to "James-Younger Gang Bank Raid," an online account by Stephanie Hess of the Northfield History Collaborative, "There was no insurance in banks in those days. If the James-Younger Gang had succeeded, the money would simply have been gone. It is possible that the 20-year-old town—including its two colleges—would not have survived."

The Golden Spike, completing the First Transcontinental Railway, was driven in 1869, so stagecoaches were increasingly out of the picture, but trains were ready to be taken. The first to get fleeced was a Rock Island Line train the gang derailed on July 21, 1873. The robbers wore Ku Klux Klan masks, perhaps as a show of their sympathies. The gang's modus operandi was to leave the passengers alone (a rarity for them) and go after the safes in the express car.

Again, the gang's great friend John Newman Edwards was there as the bandits' in-house publicist, claiming that leaving the passengers their money was proof of their robbing only the rich. (The give-to-the-poor part never actually materialized—they kept all the money they stole.)

A network of former Confederates served as the gang's support network in Missouri, and it aided them in their battle against the Pinkertons. Three officers were killed, though one of them took out John Younger in the process. This toll made the case personal for Allan Pinkerton, the Scottish immigrant and former Chicago police detective (with abolitionist sympathies) who'd begun pursuing the James Gang in 1871.

The Northfield, Minnesota, robbers' target. Luckily, they failed to get away, because a successful theft could have bankrupted the town and its two colleges. (Northfield History Collaborative)

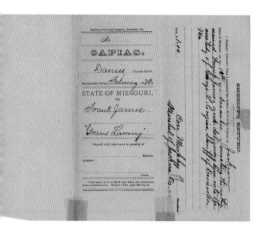

An indictment of Frank James, Missouri, 1884.

The lawmen didn't always play by the rules, either. In 1875 they threw a flare into the Samuel home, killing the James boys' half brother, Archie, and wounding their mother, Zerelda Samuel (a fierce defender of both her sons and the Confederate cause). Zerelda's hand was later amputated, but she lived until 1911. Pinkerton denied that arson was his intent, but Ted Yeatman, author of *Frank and Jesse James: The Story Behind the Legend*, uncovered a letter from Pinkerton announcing his plans to "burn the house down."

Despite Edwards' pious statements, passengers were hardly immune from the James brothers' guns. In 1881, the gang held up a Chicago, Rock Island & Pacific train in Winston, Missouri. Jesse, who never felt the need to make positive identifications before blazing away, shot the conductor dead thinking erroneously that he'd helped the Pinkertons fire bomb his family home. When a passenger tried to intervene to save the man, he too was shot and killed. All for $650.

It's interesting to point out that the late Yeatman got into a war of words with another James biographer, T.J. Stiles, whose biography *Jesse James: Last Rebel of the Civil War* made a strong case that James never stopped fighting for the Confederate cause.

Yeatman wrote, "Just where did you find an account that positively identified Jesse James as the killer of Sheets in the Gallatin robbery of Dec. 1869? Also, have you ever seen the manuscript copies of the letters Jesse sent to the various newspapers? I sure haven't, and no one that I know has."

There is, in fact, some speculation that John Newman Edwards was the ghost writer of the letters he published and attributed to the pen of Jesse James. But it can't be proven one way or the other at this point.

THE DEATH OF JESSE JAMES

From here it was all anticlimactic. Since it was hot for them in Missouri, Frank and Jesse relocated to Nashville, Tennessee, where they went under the names Thomas Howard (Jesse) and B.J. Woodson (Frank). Frank was willing to lead a quieter life, but Jesse formed a new gang that, once again, struck in Missouri, sticking up a train in what is now Independence on October 8, 1879, robbing two other trains, and going after a federal paymaster in Killen, Alabama. Stores were also pillaged in western Mississippi. A shootout in Louisiana killed two gang members.

The still-boyish Robert Ford, supposedly posing with the gun he used to kill Jesse James. (Wikipedia)

Soon there was no more gang, just Frank and Jesse. In 1881, Frank lit out for Virginia, but Jesse was only really comfortable in Missouri, and so headed back there and rented a house with his family in St. Joseph. By this point, Jesse James confided only in the Ford brothers, Charley and Robert. The former was a veteran of the James gang, but Robert was new to the fold.

It's hard to imagine that Jesse would feel safe at home in Missouri, when Missouri Governor Thomas T. Crittenden was focused on bringing him in, and there was a $5,000 bounty on each James head.

Missourian Robert Ford was born in 1862, so he knew only secondhand accounts of the Civil War. He was raised on accounts, undoubtedly florid and inaccurate, about the exploits of Jesse James. It must have been exciting for him when his older brother, Charley, joined the gang and took part in the 1881 Blue Cut robbery near Glendale, Missouri. This was the James Gang's last train robbery, and it netted $3,000 in cash and jewels—from the passengers this time.

In January 1882 two gang members—Wood Hite and Dick Liddel—were staying at the home of Bob Ford's sister, Martha Bolton, when they got into a dispute that turned violent. Hite shot Liddel in the leg, and Liddel fired back, catching Hite in the arm. Ford, who was close to Liddel, then intervened and shot Hite dead.

Robert Ford was arrested for shooting Hite, but when the authorities learned he had access to Jesse James, they secretly enlisted the governor's help and offered the young man a deal—kill Jesse James and receive a full pardon, plus the reward.

With nowhere else to turn, and trusting no one else, Jesse James planned yet another bank robbery with the Ford brothers. They were going to take out a bank in Platte City, Missouri, and worked on the plan at breakfast meeting at James' home in St. Joseph. When Jesse noticed that a framed needlepoint picture was crooked, he lined up a chair to straighten it out. That's when Bob Ford saw his chance and fatally shot Jesse James—then only thirty-four—just behind his right ear.

Cue the nineteenth-century folk song, "Jesse James," about "the dirty little coward" who "laid Jesse James in his grave." Initially, both Fords were charged with murdering both Wood Hite and Jesse James, and they were actually sentenced to hang. But true to his word, Governor Crittenden pardoned Charley and Robert Ford. The Fords capitalized on their fame, and though they

Top: This photo, disputed by some, is said to show Robert Ford (left) with the man he killed, Jesse James. (Lois Gibson)

Bottom: Robert Ford shoots Jesse James while he's hanging a picture, earning him the "coward" epithet that dogged the rest of his days. (Wikipedia)

received only part of their reward (some say only $600), additional funds came when they starred in a joint stage act called *Outlaws of Missouri*.

Charley Ford, who lived in fear of being tracked down by Frank James, relocated, became a drug addict, and changed his name several times, but, apparently unable to continue, committed suicide in 1884. Bob moved to Creede, Colorado, and in 1892 opened the Ford's Exchange dance hall. The building, along with the rest of the downtown, burned down six days later.

Ford was operating his makeshift saloon out of a tent on May 29, 1892, when in walked Edward O'Kelley. He said, "Hello, Bob," then let Jesse James' killer have it with both barrels of a sawed-off shotgun. Ron Hansen's book *The Assassination of Jesse James by the Coward Robert Ford* dramatizes the moment:

> The shotgun ignited once and again from five away, clumped sprays of shrapnel ripping into the man's neck and jawbone, ripping through his carotid artery and jugular vein, stripping skin away, and nailing the gold collar button into scantling wood. His body jolted backward, jolted the floorboards, and Ella Mae Waterson screamed, but Robert Ford only looked at the ceiling, the light going out of his eyes before he could say the right words.

Buried in Creede, the body was later dug up and replanted in Richmond, Missouri, his hometown. O'Kelley got twenty years, served ten, and was on the streets of Oklahoma City in 1904 when he was shot dead by the authorities. Nobody connected to Jesse James prospered from the link.

Nobody, that is, except Frank James. He surrendered in 1882 at Jefferson City, Missouri, but served jail time only awaiting trial. Again, newspaperman Edwards was pulling strings to make things as easy as possible for the James gang.

Frank James was acquitted of the two murder-robberies he was charged with, though he was long Jesse James' comrade-in-arms and sometimes leader of the gang. In later years, Frank James sold shoes, took tickets at a St. Louis burlesque theater, and lectured occasionally. With partners, he invested in "Buckskin Bill's Wild West Show," an imitation of Buffalo Bill's much larger operation. At the end of his life he was back at the family homestead, giving tours for twenty-five cents each. He died in 1915 at age seventy-two.

Left: Jesse in his coffin. (Library of Congress)

Right: Frank James in later life. He became respectable. (Library of Congress)

Bottom: The house in St. Joseph, Missouri, where Robert Ford shot Jesse James, with the bullet hole a tourist attraction today. (Library of Congress)

Between 1866 and 1882, according to the *Missouri Historical Review*, the James boys had been involved in bank robberies in Liberty, Lexington, Savannah, Richmond, Gallatin, and Saint Genevieve in Missouri; in Kentucky's Russellville and Columbia; and in Corydon, Iowa. They had held up the cashier of the Kansas City fair association and robbed trains near Council Bluffs, Iowa and Gads Hill, Missouri. A number of the crimes left dead men behind.

It's a pity the story of Jesse James ended the way it did, with a shot from behind, because it offered ripe material for a new framing of the story that obscured the brothers' violent, racist past. As the *Missouri Review*'s William A. Settle, Jr., writes, "It is only natural that the inability of Missouri officers to capture the outlaws, the questionable methods which brought an end to the career of outlawry, and Frank's final release would have their repercussions on the politics of the state." And not necessarily in a good way.

WHERE THEY WENT BAD

The brutalities of the Civil War turned Jesse James into something of a monster. Had it not intervened so decisively in his family's affairs he might have indeed followed early inclinations and become a minister and model citizen. But he eventually came to justify any crime, no matter how horrific, as payback for the perceived injustices of the Reconstruction period. His fellow travelers became Klan members and, in period photographs, are seen in the front rows of lynching parties.

WHAT THEY SAID

Jesse James—in a signed letter that appeared in Nashville's *Republican Banner* of July 6, 1875, and was reprinted in the *New York Times*—wrote:

> I ask space in your valuable paper to say a few words in my defence...I have never been out of Missouri since the Amnesty Bill was introduced into the Mo. Legislature asking for the pardon of the James and Youngers...There are hundreds of people in Mo. who will swear that I have never been in Ky.

They be desperadoes raving around in Ky., and it is probily very important
for the Officials of Ky to be very vigilant.

James, if he actually wrote the letter, was denying reports that he had committed
crimes in Kentucky. But he certainly did—on May 20, 1868, Jesse and Cole Younger
relieved a bank in Russellville, Kentucky of $9,035.92. On their way out of town, the
gang shot a hole in the fish-themed weather vane atop the courthouse. The vane, still
with the hole, now adorns the new courthouse.

From Major John N. Edwards' 1877 *Noted Guerrillas: Warfare of the Border*:

> No man ever strove harder to put the past behind him [than did Jesse
> James]. No man ever submitted more sincerely to the result of a war. No
> man ever went to work with a heartier good will to keep good faith with
> society and make himself amenable to the law . . . . He was not permitted so
> to do, try how he would, and as hard, and as patiently.

"Bob Ford I don't trust; I think he is a sneak. But Charlie Ford is as true as steel."
This was quoted by Frank Triplett in his 1882 biography, compiled from contemporary
newspaper accounts and attributed to Jesse James.

Teresa O'Neill, series editor of *The American Frontier, Opposing Viewpoints*, said, "An
examination of a photograph of the real-life Jesse James reveals someone who more
resembles a serial killer than he does Tyrone Power or Robert Wagner."

Jesse James, Jr., in his biography of his father, said,

> Hundreds of different books have been written and published about Jesse
> James, and what is commonly known as 'The James Band.' Many of these
> books were false from cover to cover. A few had in them a grain or two
> of truth upon which were strung whole chapters of untruths. I have read
> them all, and there is not one of them that did not do cruel injustice to the
> memory of my father and to his family . . . . I defy the world to show that
> he ever slew a human being except in the protection of his own life or as a
> soldier in honorable warfare. His only brother, whose name was linked with
> his in all the years of his life, is a free man today, acquitted of all crime.

THE BLOODY ESPINOSAS

(ALL DIED 1863)

EARLY SERIAL KILLERS

APPALL-O-METER: 10

THE BLOODY ESPINOSAS

An artist's conception of Felipe Espinosa.

THE LEGEND

The Espinosa brothers, Felipe Nerio and his younger brother, Jose Vivian, plus a young nephew, are poorly remembered today, but a legend did grow up around them after all three were killed in 1863. Violent they were, the story goes (with thirty-two dead, how could they argue otherwise?), but the killings were an inevitable response to the poor treatment of Mexican-Americans in Northern New Mexico after the Treaty of Guadalupe Hidalgo was signed, ending the Mexican-American War of 1846 to 1848.

HOW THEY GET IT WRONG

The error here is the same as it is with John Wesley Hardin and Jesse James. It can be convenient to turn bandits into conscious political actors, and it's done all the time in the popular literature. But the violence in all three cases seemed to be blood for blood's sake—Hardin killed a man for snoring (or says he did), James killed unarmed bank clerks for no reason, and the Bloody Espinosas, well, they may have been America's first serial killers. And their victims were Hispanic as well as Anglo.

WHAT WE ACTUALLY KNOW

New Mexico was in turmoil in the postwar period. This was the time of manifest destiny, and President James K. Polk was able to use the one-sided conflict, which began with border skirmishes, to further his aims of expanding the new American nation to the Pacific Ocean. As History.net reports in its "Mexican-American War" article, "When the dust cleared, Mexico had lost about one-third of its territory, including nearly all of present-day California, Utah, Nevada, Arizona and New Mexico."

Although the treaty stated that Hispanic residents would retain their property rights, the New Mexico Office of the State Historian reports, "Some entrepreneurial Americans implemented a process of chicanery and manipulation of the system that caused the Hispano people to lose two thirds of their common lands to the new conquerors. Felipe Nerio and his family were among those who lost land." In addition, six Espinosa family members had been killed during the war when the U.S. Navy shelled Vera Cruz, Mexico.

A series of unfamiliar rules and taxes were imposed on the Hispanic population, and further consternation was caused by one Archibald Gillespie (a veteran of the Mexican-American war), who'd been sent to Colorado by President Polk to perform a census—which the local population thought was in preparation for their being drafted into the army. The scene was set for a tax revolt that the new U.S. regime was inclined to repress with force.

One of five siblings, Felipe Nerio, was born in approximately 1836 to Pedro Ygnacio Espinosa and Maria Gertrudis Chavez in San Juan Nepomuceno de El Rito, New Mexico. His brother, Jose Vivian, was born circa 1846.

In 1858, Pedro Espinosa and his wife, Secundina Hurtado, moved the family to San Rafael, Colorado. They were in search of sufficient land to eke out a living, and it's not surprising that both parents and sons were resentful about what they'd lost in New Mexico. It was around this time that Felipe and Jose Espinosa began to steal horses and rob freight wagons. They weren't murderers—yet—but they soon would be.

A LIFE OF CRIME

A military detachment was sent from Fort Garland to San Rafael to arrest the Espinosas, who were part of the tax revolt and had been recognized in New Mexico during the robbing of a wagon belonging to a local priest. The driver was horrifically mutilated during this incident, but he survived to tell the law where to find the brothers. The confrontation with the military didn't go peacefully. A shootout left an American corporal dead. The brothers escaped into the Sangre de Cristo Mountains and reportedly returned home to find their property burned and ransacked.

Descendant Martin Edward Martinez claimed that the Espinosas only became killers after American soldiers actually killed family members and raped their wives and daughters. Needless to say, that hasn't been verified. Martinez wrote in a thesis, quoted in a Legends of America report: "The Bloody Espinosas—Terrorizing Colorado":

> The story of the Espinosas unveils the hardship and the terror that they faced when the soldiers, frontiersmen, pioneers and setters came after the Mexican and American war . . . . If the Espinosas were bandits, guerrilla fighters and killers, let the truth be known. If the Espinosas were fighting for justice, let it be known. The Espinosas could even have been heroes.

What we do know is that Felipe Espinosa claimed to have had a vision from the Virgin Mary directing him to kill one hundred gringos for every family member he lost in the war, which would have been 600 people in total. He drew up a "Statement of Principles" for Colorado Governor John Evans, demanding full pardons of him and his men, as well as 5,000 acres of land and appointment to the Colorado Volunteers. Felipe certainly did not lack for chutzpah, and he made every effort to put his plan into action.

The first of the victims unlucky enough to get in the brothers' way was found in March of 1863 in the Arkansas River country, hacked and mutilated (with a crucifix of twigs sticking out of his head). He was a blameless farmer named Franklin William Bruce. From there, according to Charles F. Price in his book *Season of Terror: The*

Espinosas in Central Colorado, the brothers went a few miles north and murdered a sawmill worker, Henry Harkens, who was left with his head split open via a hatchet. Then the brothers went even further north into South Park, and this time they found and killed a mail station operator named John Addleman.

A rare survivor of an encounter with the Espinosas was a lumberman named Matthew Metcalfe. He was driving a wagon full of logs through California Gulch in South Park when he ran straight into an Espinosa ambush. A bullet hit Metcalfe in the left breast, and he fell backwards onto his timber, but he didn't die—a copy of Abraham Lincoln's January 1863 "Emancipation Proclamation" in his shirt pocket kept him alive to describe the brothers.

Colonel John Chivington was sent after the Bloody Espinosas by Territorial Governor John Evans. He was later implicated in the infamous Sand Creek Massacre. (Wikipedia)

Bodies were found with their hearts cut out, or crucifixes cut into their chests. *Season of Terror* reports that after the first five unexplained murders, there was speculation that either guerrillas or jayhawkers (antislavery militants from Kansas) were involved. Early suspicion that Native Americans were to blame was quickly dispelled because none were known to be hostile.

According to Price in an interview with *Westword* newspaper, South Park was then a busy gold-mining region "and they killed six men there at different times and committed pretty horrible butcheries at the same time they killed these people. One of the men that they killed was the brother of an officer in the first Colorado cavalry." This led to the cavalry being sent in, and they "combined with some of the more dangerous members of the South Park community—and some lynch mobs hanged a few people thinking they were the Espinosas, but they weren't."

On May 9, 1863, the Espinosa brothers were tracked down by a posse (Price says they were self-appointed) out of Park County, Colorado, to a location near Canon City,

Colorado. They ambushed the gang and killed Jose Vivian, but Felipe—the man of visions—got away.

The Rocky Mountain News Weekly was ecstatic that the gang—or at least half of it—had been brought to ground. "The people of California Gulch are entitled to a great deal of credit for the zeal they displayed in ridding the country of a desperado, and having performed the labor and spent the time necessary for that object it is no more than fair that other localities should stand the expense incurred."

Doubtlessly distraught over the loss of his brother and partner in crime, Felipe wasn't ready to surrender. Instead he brought a fifteen-year-old nephew on board—keeping it in the family—and killed a couple more people, including a man and his wife. What was left of the gang went back to the Sangre de Cristo Mountains where they committed further heinous acts.

THE SPREE GOES FREE-FORM

Their next victim was a woman, Maria Dolores Sánches, proving that their crime spree had become free-form and was not exclusively centered on gringos. (Or perhaps she was fair game because she was traveling with a gringo.)

As Price tells it, Sánches was making her way across the Sangre de Cristo Pass on October 8, 1863, as she traveled from Trinidad to Costilla, New Mexico Territory. Driving the mule-drawn buggy was a man named Philbrook. He was one of two brothers originally from Maine, Leander D. or Henry Clay—history fails to record which one. The middle brother, Darius, had been killed the year before by a military firing squad, accused of trying to kill a superior officer.

The relationship between Sánches and Philbrook isn't clear—perhaps she was an employee or a housekeeper, or maybe more. Entering a canyon, the pair heard four shots, one of which killed a mule. Philbrook unhitched the dead mule and attempted to flee with the surviving one, but that one was shot dead, too. The pair jumped out of the wagon, dodging bullets, and ran into the mountains. The bandits took down the luggage from the buggy and set it on fire.

Sánches remained concealed until she heard another wagon approaching, driven by a Mexican named Pedro Garcia. She jumped out and he concealed her in his wagon, but a short distance later, the Espinosa pair jumped out with guns drawn. Charles F. Price's *Season of Terror: The Espinosas in Central Colorado*, quotes Tom Tobin, the tracker who would eventually take out Felipe Espinosa, as saying that Sánches was spotted, after which Felipe declared, "Put that prostitute of the American out of the wagon or we will fire on you." Not wanting to get Garcia killed, Sánches complied, and the two murderers (described later by Garcia as a man and a boy) told the driver to move on.

The times didn't permit detailed accounts of sexual abuse, but Tobin says the pair "abused her disgracefully." Amazingly, after Sánches was tied up she managed to chew through her restraints and escape. She was almost taken captive again and refused passage by some travelers afraid of reprisals from the Espinosas, but her ordeal was almost over. Philbrook made it to Fort Garland, stated his case to Colonel Sam Tappan, and joined a rescue party that caught up with Sánches about eight miles from Fort Garland. This was a rare case in which both intended victims of the Espinosas lived to tell the tale. Garcia survived, too.

TRACKED BY TOM TOBIN

But the two remaining Espinosas, with a $2,500 bounty on their heads, were not long for this world. Colonel Tappan employed the services of a well-regarded mountain man, trapper, tracker, and scout named Tom Tate Tobin to administer the *coup de grace*.

Tobin, an associate of Kit Carson (and later father-in-law to Carson's son) was offered a detachment of fifteen soldiers, but they mostly just slowed the tracker down. The soldiers hadn't seen Tobin's like before—he allowed only a few hours of sleep a night and refused to permit cooking fires. Anyone who complained was sent back to the fort. Tobin located the Espinosas on the fourth day. He shot them both with a Hawken muzzleloader. Felipe's last words were, "Jesus, favor me!" With both dead, Tobin cut off their heads, bagged them, and brought them back to Fort Garland. Their reign of terror, which had claimed thirty-two lives, was over.

Asked how the search had gone when he returned to the fort, Tobin said, according to Price's book, "So so" and rolled the two heads out on the floor. The reeking relics were later sent to Washington, D.C., where they were ill-received. Perhaps this is why Tobin received only $1,500 and not the full reward. He got a Kit Carson-style coat from the governor of Colorado and a Henry rifle from the Army. Tappan paid some money to Tobin himself and much later helped the elderly and penniless man get some financial relief.

Thomas Tate Tobin in full regalia as a tracker. He got his men, and had the heads to prove it. (Wikipedia)

WHERE THEY WENT BAD

Perhaps the Espinosas would have remained peaceable farmers had they not been dispossessed from their land in New Mexico, but there was clearly something wrong with Felipe from an early age. Tobin's biographer, James E. Perkins, asserts that Felipe was by nature both violent and mentally unstable, and possibly criminally insane. He had a short fuse, and it was lit early in life.

WHAT THEY SAID

John McCannon, part of the posse responsible for killing Jose Vivian, found a letter written to Governor Evans among the effects the fleeing Felipe Espinosa left behind in his hasty escape. The self-serving letter is almost pathologically delusional:

> They ruined our families—they took everything in our house, first our beds and blankets, then our provisions. Seeing this, we said, 'We would rather be dead than see such infamies committed on our families.' These were the reasons we had to go out and kill Americans—revenge for the infamies committed on our families. But we have repented of killing. Pardon us for what we have done and give us our liberty so that no officer will have anything to do with us, for also in killing, one gains his liberty. I am aware that you know of some I have killed, but of others you don't know. It is a sufficient number, however. Ask in New Mexico if any other two men have killed as many men as the Espinosas. We have killed 32.

BUTCH CASSIDY AND THE SUNDANCE KID

(1866-1908) (1867-1908)

MADE BY THE MOVIES

APPALL-O-METER: 5

BUTCH CASSIDY
AND THE SUNDANCE KID

THE LEGEND

The chances are overwhelming that Harry Alonzo Longabaugh "The Sundance Kid" and Butch Cassidy would be complete unknowns today had not screenwriter William Goldman been taken by their story. He liked the fact that the partners got second acts in their lives. After almost running out their string in the Old West, they fled to South America, first Argentina and then Bolivia.

And while they didn't exactly reinvent themselves—they were still thieves—they wrote a new ending to their story. Of course, this is exactly the part of the script that the Hollywood executives tried to change. It may have been what actually happened, but audiences weren't supposed to like "heroes" who ran from a fight.

But this was 1969 and the age of the antihero, so George Roy Hill's film, *Butch Cassidy and the Sundance Kid*, about two lovable rogues hit a chord. The movie took in $45 million, and it had company in advancing leading men and women who had dark dimensions to them. Warren Beatty turned down the Sundance Kid role because he thought the character was too much like Clyde Barrow from *Bonnie and Clyde*. On deck was Robert Altman's 1971 *McCabe and Mrs. Miller*, a downbeat Western that did work for Beatty.

Parker's cattle thefts could have a touch of Robin Hood about them, in the context that the big ranchers were then squeezing the small ones out of business. But, once again, there's no evidence that Parker and his gang preyed only on large spreads, and they definitely didn't redistribute their ill-gotten goods.

Butch Cassidy and his friend Harry Longabaugh weren't legends in their own time— they were legends in ours.

The movie made Butch Cassidy and Harry Longabaugh (aka The Sundance Kid) far more famous than they were in life. But Etta Place remains a mystery. (20th Century Fox)

HOW THEY GET IT WRONG

It's a die-hard silver screen trope, but criminals tend to be antisocial and are seldom endearing. Onscreen, this pair was relatable, brave, funny, charming, and not overly violent. In reality, they were just average bad guys, albeit ones with their passports stamped. The foreign adventures set them apart. Most of the black hats I'm writing about here met their end much too close to home.

WHAT WE ACTUALLY KNOW

Let's start with the bowler-hatted Robert Leroy Parker, aka Butch Cassidy. He looks extremely pleased with himself in the few surviving photos and is dressed like a city dude. But unlike Longabaugh, he was a real Westerner, born circa 1866 in Beaver, Utah, to emigrants from Britain named Maximillian Parker and Ann Campbell Gillies.

They may have been transplants, arriving separately in the 1850s, but Parker and Gillies adopted quickly to their new home. In 1879 they moved across the mountains to Circleville, and Roy (as he was then known) found work at the many ranches in the area. There was early evidence of criminal intent—Parker broke into a store and stole a pair of jeans (though he promised to come back later and settle up).

The owner of those jeans pressed charges, but young Parker was acquitted. According to Larry Pointer's *In Search of Butch Cassidy*, the teenage outlaw-in-the-making "had been raised with the frontier ethic that a man's word was his bond. The IOU was an inviolate pledge. The merchant's distrust was an unfamiliar response and, before the matter was settled, the humiliated youth was having mixed emotions over legal process and blind justice."

Others might have shrugged the incident, but it happened around the same time that Parker's father saw a legal dispute over property rights go against him. The law wasn't fair, Roy Parker undoubtedly concluded. And to paraphrase Merle Haggard's song "Mama Tried," it was "to the bad he kept on turning."

A FULL-TIME CRIMINAL

The nickname "Butch" (originally "Butcher") came from early work slicing up meat in Rock Springs, Wyoming. By 1884, according to Utah.com, Parker was rustling cattle from Parowan (just over the Markagunt Plateau) and modeling himself on a rustling rancher whose alias was Mike Cassidy. Roy Parker became Butch Cassidy, the criminal. Other accounts doubt the Mike Cassidy angle, since the rancher (whose real name was J.T. McClammy) would have been too young at the time to be a mentor to Butch Cassidy.

Moving west to Telluride, Butch Cassidy met another bad hat, Matt Warner, owner of a racehorse. They campaigned the horse locally, but they had their eyes on bigger targets. Cassidy began his criminal career in earnest with a stickup of the San Miguel Valley Bank in Telluride on June 24, 1889.

Warner recruited Cassidy and Tom McCarty, his own brother-in-law. The robbery was successful, despite the fact that the novice criminals brought the teller outside with his hands up, thus alerting the whole town. The robbers got away with $21,000 (in today's dollars, $516,000) then took off with the loot to a hideout called the Robbers Roost in southeastern Utah. Cassidy used some of the loot to buy land, ostensibly operated as a ranch, near Dubois, Wyoming. It was conveniently close to Hole-in-the-Wall, a forbidding rock formation that, like Robbers Roost, was used as a hideout. (Many years later, actor Paul Newman, who played Cassidy in the film, would establish the Hole in the Wall Gang Camp in Connecticut for children with serious illnesses.)

The ranch was a front for cattle and horse rustling, and it was for the latter crime that Cassidy was convicted in 1894. He got two years in the Wyoming State Prison and served eighteen months.

BUTCH CASSIDY MEETS THE SUNDANCE KID

The case for Cassidy includes the fact that, although he liked to wave guns around when committing his robberies, he wasn't trigger happy and was proud of the fact that he never killed anyone. The same could not be said for all of his associates, who after Cassidy got out of jail formed the famous "Wild Bunch." Though the movie depicts Cassidy as best friends with the Sundance Kid, he was actually closer in the gang to William Ellsworth "Elzy" Lay.

Opposite: A young Butch Cassidy. (Library of Congress)

Above: The Wild Bunch (aka Hole in the Wall Gang) included, sitting left to right, Harry Longabaugh/Sundance, Ben Kilpatrick and Robert Leroy Parker (aka Butch Cassidy). Standing are Will "News" Carver and Harvey Logan (aka Kid Curry).

The next hit was on August 13, 1896, when the Wild Bunch cleaned out the bank in Montpelier, Idaho, of $7,000. And this is where Harry Longabaugh comes into the picture. The story is that Cassidy, who was still seeing Annie Bassett and hiding out at the Robbers Roost, recruited him.

Mark Smokov's *He Rode with Butch and Sundance: The Story of Harvey (Kid Curry) Logan*, citing historian Ed Bartholomew, asserts that it was "romantic mythmaking" and Hollywood hyperbole that claimed Butch Cassidy ran the Wild Bunch. According to the book, Logan and Will "News" Carver were the actual leaders. The gang-chasing lawman Joe LeFors only cites Cassidy by name once in his own book, and The Sundance Kid not at all.

Charles Siringo, a Pinkerton detective who likewise pursued the gang, also barely mentions Sundance in his memoirs. And he leaves Cassidy out of some of the major train robberies. In fact, says Smokov, "There is no concrete evidence that [Cassidy] ever led or participated in any train robbery, this was Kid Curry's specialty." Siringo calls the robbers the "Kid Curry Gang," though he does describe Cassidy as "the shrewdest and most daring outlaw of the present age."

The Pleasant Valley Coal Company's payroll was taken for another $7,000 in gold on April 22, 1897, at Castle Gate, Utah. Events took a darker turn for the gang. On June 2, 1899, (the dawn of the automotive age it might be noted) the Wild Bunch robbed a Union Pacific Overland Flyer passenger train in Wilcox, Wyoming. After that raid, Kid Curry and George Curry got into a gun battle with lawmen and killed Sheriff Joe Hazen. That elevated their crimes, and the Pinkertons, who were pretty good at what they did, got called in. But there was more bloodshed to come.

On July 11, 1899, the gang hit a Colorado and Southern Railroad train in Folsom, New Mexico. In an ensuing shootout, Elzy Lay killed Sheriff Edward Far and Henry Love. He was caught, convicted, and sent to the New Mexico State Penitentiary for life. Keep in mind that Lay and Cassidy were close, so while he may have personally abstained from violence, he sure was close to it. Cassidy was said to have planned this particular train robbery.

Trigger-happy gang member Elzy Lay killed two lawmen and was sent to the New Mexico State Penitentiary for life. (Glade Ross Collection)

Despite an aborted attempt to gain amnesty in 1899 by pledging not to rob any more trains, the gang kept on with their intended line of work, and more lawmen died. Curry and News Carver fled from a posse in Apache Country, Arizona, killing Deputies Andrew Gibbons and Frank LeSueur in the process. By this point, not much separated the gang from later criminal enterprises featuring John Dillinger, "Machine Gun" Kelly, and "Pretty Boy" Floyd. The technology, both in weaponry and transportation, just got better.

Blood was shed on both sides. George Curry was shot dead on April 17, 1900, after which Kid Curry took out his killers, Utah Sheriff John Tyler and Deputy

Opposite: The San Miguel Valley Bank was an early target of the gang in 1889. (Wikipedia)

Sam Jenkins. A few months later, on August 29, Butch Cassidy, the Sundance Kid, and their associates robbed Union Pacific Train #3 near Tipton, Wyoming, of a whopping $55,000. This alone would have set the gang up for life, but they kept at it, fleecing the First National Bank of Winnemucca, Nevada, of $32,640 on September 19, 1900.

A few months later the gang posed for a famous photograph in Fort Worth, Texas. It features Longabaugh, Cassidy, Kid Curry, "News" Carver, and Ben Kilpatrick. Since they could easily have slipped across the border and lived large on their takings, the gang seemed to be robbing trains and banks for the thrill of it at this point. Their total take was the equivalent of millions today.

Yet another train, a Great Northern, was attacked near Wagner, Montana, on July 3, 1901, and $60,000 in cash taken. A posse then caught up with News Carver and ended his days as a train robber (or anything else for that matter).

Ben Kilpatrick was captured, but Kid Curry (portrayed in the movie as dim-witted, but actually quite sharp) kept on killing people, including Knoxville, Tennessee, policemen William Dinwiddle and Robert Saylor. In Montana, he murdered rancher James Winters.

SOUTH AMERICAN INTERLUDE

The Sundance Kid kept company with a woman named Etta Place. Not much is known about her, though a surviving photograph shows her to be quite pretty (and looking not unlike Katharine Ross, who played her in the movie—including in the famous bicycle-riding "Raindrops Keep Falling on My Head" sequence). Place may have been a prostitute, or a school teacher, or neither one. Her real name isn't even clear; she called herself Ethel.

There's even speculation that Etta Place was the same woman as Annie Bassett, who was reportedly Cassidy's lover. In this version, she'd have had to keep company with both men. Cassidy was said to have visited the Bassett family's Colorado ranch, Brown's Park (a known haven for bandits), in 1889. "I thought he was the most dashing and handsome

Opposite: Kid Curry (aka Harvey Logan) with Annie Rogers (aka Della Moore). (Wikipedia)

BUTCH AND THE BOX OFFICE

How big was *Butch Cassidy and the Sundance Kid*? Boffo! According to Box Office Mojo, the 1969 hit took in $102,308,889. The Fox release was the 700th biggest-grossing domestic film of all time. When the receipts are adjusted for ticket price inflation, Butch comes in at 39th, ahead of *Independence Day*, *Home Alone*, and *Love Story*.

Critics didn't like *Butch* at first—however, its reputation grew. Roger Ebert called it "slow and disappointing," and Gene Siskel said it was "too cute to be believed . . . not memorable." A take of over $100 million made them kinder about it, and now it glows, despite what Michael Phillips in *The Chicago Tribune* calls "the sardonic mutterings of William Goldman's Oscar-winning screenplay," which "may not have been period-accurate, but the in-authenticity was part of the joke, and the charm."

According to *The Hollywood Story* by Joel Waldo Finler, Fox recorded losses of more than $100 million for 1969-1970, so *Butch Cassidy and the Sundance Kid* (along with *M*A*S*H**) arguably saved the studio from the disaster of *Hello Dolly!*, *Tora! Tora! Tora!*, And *The Only Game in Town*. Films with exclamation points were bad for the studio.

man I had ever seen," Bassett is quoted as saying in *Wild Bunch Women* by Michael Rutter. "I was such a young thing, and looked upon Butch as my knight in shining armor." She says it annoyed her no end that he seemed more interested in his horse than her, but eventually they got together. "I didn't let him get bored," she said.

Computer testing of photographs suggests that Place and Bassett may have been one and the same, but it's hardly conclusive, and there are times when Place was in South America that Bassett was definitely seen in the U.S. Unlike the mysterious Etta Place, we know a fair amount about Annie Bassett, who lived until 1956. She never claimed to be Etta Place, even in her memoirs.

What we do know is that Butch Cassidy, the Sundance Kid, and a woman calling herself Etta (or Ethel) Place decided things had gotten too hot in the United States, what with the Pinkertons closing in, so in 1901 they boarded a ship for South America. Far from disowning Kid Curry's many murders, they tried to get him to go along. According to *What They Didn't Teach You About the Wild West* by Mike Wright, they took "$30,000 in ill-gotten

Opposite: Etta Place and Harry Longabaugh. Was that her real name, or was it Annie Bassett? (GL Archive/Alamy Stock Photo)

Above: Laura Bullion was another associate of the Wild Bunch. She was romantically involved with Ben Kilpatrick (known as "The Tall Texan"), and in 1901 got five years for her part in the Great Northern train robbery. (Wikipedia)

gains" along with them, though given their takes through the years you think it could have been more.

Their initial destination was not Bolivia (as it is in the movie) but, aboard the British ship *Herminius*, to Argentina. They hightailed it down to Argentinian Patagonia, a fact cited by Bruce Chatwin in his groundbreaking *In Patagonia*. Chatwin even travels to the remote cabin then occupied by the trio, and finds it occupied by a Chilean Indian woman. If they'd known what was good for them, they would have stayed there.

In Argentina, Sundance and Place were Mr. and Mrs. Harry "Enrique" Place, and Cassidy was James "Santiago" Ryan. For a time, they ranched successfully in the Cholila Valley and even welcomed the territorial governor, Julio Lezana, who came by and stayed the night at their humble home, dancing with Etta/Ethel in the process.

The Pinkertons hadn't given up, however, and only the rainy season during 1903 prevented them from descending on Cholila. They put up wanted posters instead. The Pinkertons certainly noticed when a pair of English-speaking gringos held up the Banco de Tarapacá y Argentino in Rio Gallegos, 700 miles from Cholila. Governor Lezana, no longer so chummy, issued an order for Butch and Sundance's arrest. But they were tipped off by a friendly Welshman and caught the steamer to Chile.

They returned to Argentina in 1905, and with local help they stole 12,000 pesos from the Banco de la Nación in Villa Mercedes, and then fled back to Chile. Around this time, Ethel/Etta decided she'd had enough of the outdoor life, and Sundance accompanied her back to the United States. The trail goes cold on her after that.

Butch Cassidy, still traveling with the Sundance Kid, was by then trying to settle down as a rancher in Bolivia. It's unclear if the pair committed robberies in Bolivia, though some sources say they did. They also did legitimate work for a tin mining company. Ironically, their duties included guarding payrolls.

The pair definitely did hijack a Bolivian payroll for the Aramayo mines in 1908, confronting a traveling party with new Mauser carbines. Bandanas masked their faces and their hat brims were turned down—the classic TV holdup attire. The take was smaller than they expected.

A DISPUTED END

A posse was on the Americans' tail and caught up with them at the home of Bonifacio Casasola. They asked their hosts about the road to the Argentinian border. The soldiers positioned themselves on the house's patio and started firing. "Three screams of desperation" were heard from within by a witness quoted in the official inquest, then it was quiet. The next morning the soldiers entered the house and found both Yankees dead. Butch had a bullet to the head, and Sundance, on a bench behind the door, was hit in the arm and forehead.

One theory, supposedly based on an examination of the bullet in Sundance's head, claimed that Cassidy killed his partner and then himself to avoid capture. The bodies were buried at the San Vicente cemetery, near the final resting place of a German immigrant named Gustav Zimmer. This theory is probably what happened.

But, as is often the case, there are questions. Cassidy's sister asserted that her brother had survived, returned to the U.S., and lived until 1935. Josie Bassett (Annie's sister) claimed a visit from Cassidy in the 1920s. She told author Kerry Ross Boren in a 1960 interview at her home in Jensen, Utah, that Cassidy "died in Johnnie, Nevada . . . . He was an old man when he died. He had been living in Oregon, and back east for a long time, where he worked for a railroad." Another report had him driving a Model T Ford, living in the Northwest and dying in 1937.

Yet another popular theory has Butch Cassidy never going to Bolivia at all but returning from Argentina in 1908, adopting the name William T. Phillips, and living to 1937 (a married man) in Spokane, Washington. This theory is seconded by Butch's sister, Lula, who said in her 1975 book *Butch Cassidy, My Brother* that he returned home and visited the family in 1925. Handwriting analysts said the signatures matched, but other evidence suggested that William Phillips was instead William Wilcox, another outlaw.

When the film came out in 1969, a man surfaced, claiming to be the previously unknown "Harry Longabaugh, Jr." He did at least look like the Sundance Kid. To complicate matters, the bodies in the San Vicente cemetery were dug up in 1991 and found not to match up with the DNA of the dead men's descendants.

QUEEN ANN, APPROXIMATELY

Annie Bassett was known to the newspapers as Queen Ann Bassett, and both she and her sister, Josie, had wild lives. Their parents operated a successful cattle ranch in the border area of Wyoming, Colorado, and Utah. Herb Bassett moved his family to Brown's Park, Colorado, around 1888, and from that base sold horses and meat to a whole passel of outlaws. He also took in their stolen stock and sold it on to mining camps, so it was mutually beneficial.

Annie, as previously noted, claimed to have had an affair with Butch Cassidy at quite a young age. Another "associate" of hers was Ben Kilpatrick, a Wild Bunch member who continued his criminal enterprises until getting his brains bashed out during a Texas train robbery in 1912.

But Josie also left them lovelorn. Josie was involved with Cassidy's closest friend and Wild Bunch comrade, William Ellsworth "Elzy" Lay, and when he left her for Maude Davis, she moved on to News Carver (who in turn abandoned her for Laura Bullion). Josie later reportedly had something going with Butch Cassidy, too.

Both of the Bassett women were given the rare privilege of access to Wild Bunch's Robbers Roost hideout. Unless she went along as Etta Place, Annie Bassett never saw Cassidy again after he took off for South America—though Elzy Lay (who went legit as a businessman) supposedly stopped by the Bassett ranch in 1906.

Annie Bassett married Hyrum "Hi," Henry Bernard in 1903 and shortly after that was taken into custody for rustling cattle. She was acquitted. Bassett divorced Bernard and, in 1928, married another cattleman, Frank Willis. They ran a ranch in Utah and were reportedly devoted to each other. She died in Leeds, Utah, circa 1956, and if she had a secret about being Etta Place, she never shared it.

You can read more about Queen Ann in Linda Wommack's book *Ann Bassett: Colorado's Cattle Queen*. Her conclusion: Annie was not Etta.

Josie Bassett lived to be ninety. The outlaw period was a relatively brief part of a long life, but it cast a long shadow. Josie stayed on her family property and helped run the ranch. She claimed to have been visited by a very undead Butch Cassidy in 1930. She had no less than five husbands and was rumored to have poisoned the last one (a heavy drinker).

Just as Queen Ann was, Josie Bassett was accused of various criminal enterprises. These included poaching deer out of season, stealing cattle from neighbors, and, during the Depression, bootlegging. Also like Annie, Josie did well with jury trials. She was acquitted twice of cattle theft—despite hides from missing steers being found on her property.

A horse knocked Josie down in 1963, a month after John F. Kennedy was shot, and she died in 1964.

Annie Bassett may have been Etta Place, but the evidence is inconclusive. They certainly looked a lot alike. (Wikipedia)

Annie Bassett in her 70s. She never told the whole story. (Utah State Historical Society)

WHERE THEY WENT BAD

No doubt about it, Robert Leroy Parker should never have stolen that pair of jeans (and a pie!).

WHAT THEY SAID

A letter from Cassidy to friends in 1907, at age forty-one, and quoted by *Wild West* in 1997, has him saying from Bolivia: "Oh god, if I could call back 20 years . . . I would be happy." He added, "If I don't fall down I will be living here before long."

In the fall of 1899, according to another *Wild West* article, "Butch Cassidy's Surrender Offer," in 2006, Cassidy reportedly called on a prominent Utah lawyer to see about a pardon. "You're the best lawyer in Utah," he supposedly said. "You know who's who and what's what. You've got a lot of influence. I thought maybe you could fix things with the governor to give me a pardon or something so I wouldn't be bothered if I settle down and promise to go straight. I'll give you my word on it. Is there any way it could be fixed?" When told it was unlikely, and the best course was probably to leave the country, Cassidy replied, "I guess you're right, but I'm sorry it can't be fixed some way. You'll never know what it means to be forever on the dodge."

Another version of this same story, also in the 2006 *Wild West* article, has Cassidy saying:

> I'm getting sick of hiding out, always on the run and never able to stay long in one place. Now, when it comes to facts, I've kept close track of things and I know there ain't a man left in the country who can go on the stand and identify me for any crime. All of them have either died or gone away. I've been thinking, why can't I go and give myself up and stand trial on some of those old charges?

Wishful thinking there, but slightly less deluded than Felipe Espinosa.

BELLE STARR

(1848-1889)

LADIES LOVE OUTLAWS

APPALL-O-METER: 6

BELLE STARR

THE LEGEND

Far more than Pearl Hart, Belle Starr really was a bandit queen. For Hart, robbery was a one-time occurrence, but Starr stayed at it even though her no-account partners kept dying on her. The details of her crimes were hugely exaggerated in her own times by the dime novels ("the female Jesse James" or "the petticoat terror of the plains") and the *National Police Gazette* ("a wild Western amazon"). Later, Hollywood got a hold of her.

Like her contemporary in notoriety, Calamity Jane, Starr was no beauty—one contemporary description of her claims she was "hatchet-faced" and "bony and flat-chested with a mean mouth"—but she was played by beauties on the screen: Gene Tierney, Marie Windsor (a former Miss Utah), Elizabeth Montgomery, Florence Henderson, and (in the 1980 *Long Riders*) by Pamela Reed. Belle even has a cameo in a Three Stooges movie.

HOW THEY GET IT WRONG

There's not a huge paper trail on Belle Starr—she wasn't as famous as Jesse James, but what there is contains whoppers. For instance, it's frequently assumed that she had a romantic alliance with Jesse James's associate Cole Younger, and that a child resulted. This is likely untrue and was denied in Younger's autobiography. Mike Wright's *What They Didn't Teach You About the Wild West* says "the budding beauty (sic) was cultivated by a member of the Quantrill guerrilla gang, Cole Younger," and later became the common-law wife of Bruce Younger, Cole's cousin and a sometime member of the James-Younger gang. She might have had a dalliance with Bruce Younger in Kansas—it was gossip at the time—but that same year she actually married the criminally minded Sam Starr, who did little more than give her a memorable name.

Belle Starr was variously reported to have robbed banks, burned down stores, held up poker games at gunpoint, been jailed for horse theft (then taking off in the amorous embrace of her jailer), and ran a livery stable as a front for stock theft. None of it is accurate, writes historian Richard D. Arnott at History.net. "Such activities are not reflected in court records or newspaper accounts," Arnott said.

WHAT WE ACTUALLY KNOW

Even her birthplace is disputed. It is commonly believed to be Carthage, Missouri, in 1848, though Mike Wright claims it was actually Arkansas and that even her gravestone gets it wrong.

Like Pearl Hart, Starr had a relatively genteel upbringing. She was born Myra Maybelle Shirley in Carthage, which is supported by census records. Her father, John Shirley, was from a prominent Virginia family, albeit, its black sheep. John had been married and divorced twice when he hooked up with Eliza Hatfield Pennington, a Hatfield of Hatfield and McCoys fame. In southwest Missouri, where they moved in 1839, they had a prosperous farm. Later, John Shirley gave up farming and ran various successful enterprises (including an inn and a tavern) in Carthage.

Opposite: Belle Starr at Fort Smith, Arkansas, in 1886 with Deputy U.S. Marshal Benjamin Tyner Hughes. (Wikipedia)

John Shirley was civic-minded, and according to *Belle Starr and the Wild West* by Rose Blue and Corinne J. Naden, "was admired for his fine library, which contained novels, biographies and works of philosophy. The fact that he had any books at all put him in a class well above the average citizen."

Shirley helped found the Carthage Female Academy, which Myra Belle attended, learning both the piano and classical languages. She excelled at school but also enjoyed traipsing through the woods with her older brother, John Allison "Bud" Shirley. Bud was a big influence on the young woman, and when she was about twelve he taught her both how to ride horses and shoot guns.

It sounds idyllic, but the woman who was to become Belle Starr was growing up in the same Missouri-Kansas Civil War turmoil as Jesse James. John Shirley was a Quantrill enthusiast and a "hot-blooded Southerner"; he supported Bud when he joined up with the guerrilla leader and rose quickly through the ranks, attaining a captain's post. But Bud Shirley died after a house he was occupying in Sarcoxie, Missouri, was surrounded by Federals. A fleeing Shirley was shot dead trying to hop a fence.

It's not surprising that some sensational accounts have a sixteen-year-old Myra Belle vowing vengeance (as Jesse James actually did), but that's not what happened—though she may have gone on a scouting mission for her brother. The main actor was actually John Shirley, whose thriving enterprises were destroyed by the Civil War. Shirley left it all behind, gathered up his family, and headed for Scyene, Texas, where he once again farmed—this time an 800-acre land grant. He seems to have had a lot of moxie, because he soon constructed a nice new family home on what he made from selling hogs, horses, cows, and such crops as corn and sorghum.

Belle Starr and the Wild West reports that Cole Younger came to stay at the Shirley farm in 1866, and brings up the rumor that Belle's daughter Pearl (later a madam) was Younger's daughter. But the authors also cite Younger's denial—he says the visit to the Shirley farm was in 1864, when Myra Belle was only sixteen. "Belle cherished a sentimental memory of Cole Younger all her life," reports author Burton Rascoe. He adds that if the bandit queen and Younger really *were* an item, he was the only one of Belle's lovers "to die with his boots off."

Here's Younger's version, from his 1903 autobiography, *The Story of Cole Younger, by Himself*:

> One of the richest mines for the romancers who have pretended to write the story of my life was the fertile imagination of Belle Starr, who is now dead, peace to her ashes. These fairy tales have told how the 'Cherokee maiden fell in love with the dashing captain.' As a matter of fact, Belle Starr was not a Cherokee. Her father was John Shirley, who during the war had a hotel at Carthage, Missouri. In the spring of 1864, while I was in Texas, I visited her father, who had a farm near Syene, in Dallas County. Belle Shirley was then 14 (sic), and there were two or three brothers smaller.

Younger claims he next saw Myra Belle in 1868, when she was married to Jim Reed "who had been in my company during the war. This was about three months before the birth of her eldest child, Pearl Reed, afterward known as Pearl Starr, after Belle's second husband."

Younger said that he heard that Myra Belle was sweet on him, and afterwards "evaded the wife of my former comrade in arms." He adds that Myra Belle herself spread the story that Pearl was his child. "Her story was a fabrication," Younger writes. Of course, Younger could be lying, too.

BAD COMPANIONS

Myra Belle met Jim Reed in Missouri when he was running with the Confederate guerrillas. Undoubtedly, given her family background, she was impressed by that. Apparently, the family had no objections to Reed, either, and they were married in Collins County, Texas on November 1, 1866, with the Reverend S.M. Williams presiding.

Belle and Jim Reed lived with his parents in Missouri, where Pearl was born, and attended church regularly. But Jim wanted a faster life. He raced horses and began spending time with Tom Starr, a shady character given to rustling and whiskey running. He was "so notorious that he was an embarrassment to the Cherokee Nation," reports Richard Arnott in his History.net article.

Belle's brother, Edwin, was also a horse thief and was shot dead by Texas law officers in 1868. Myra Belle visited her parents in Texas for a while after the second Shirley boy was shot, but then the young family decamped for California and briefly lived in Los Angeles where they had a second child, James Edwin. Jim Reed worked in a gambling house.

Belle Reed wrote to her surviving brother, Marion, from California in 1872. She said the family was settled on Los Nietos Island. "Jimmie has bought land here on this island and I guess we will make a permanent home here. I am perfectly satisfied."

It wasn't to be—Jim Reed was accused of passing counterfeit money (some say bad checks), and Belle fled back to Texas, with the family following. Jim was now rarely at home and started spending all his time with Tom Starr and his fellow thieves. In February 1873, Reed was reportedly part of a gang of four who robbed and killed a man named Dick Cravery. Another murder, of a former gang member, followed. Jim escaped to Indian Territory, taking Belle with him but leaving the two children with her parents in Scyene.

No, he didn't go straight. The Watt Grayson family was robbed of $30,000 on November 19, 1873. Grayson and his wife were hung from a tree until they disclosed the location of their money. Some say Belle was involved in this crime, but if so, she would have been disguised as a man.

Opposite: Starr in full regalia as a friend and accomplice of the outlaws. (Pictorial Press Ltd/Alamy Stock Photo)

At this point Jim and Belle split up, but not because she objected to his life of crime and murder. However, she most definitely *did* object to his taking up with another woman, Rosa McCommas. Belle returned to her family in Texas. Jim Reed went on terrorizing the countryside until he was shot dead near Paris, Texas, by law enforcement authorities in August of 1874.

The stories of Belle robbing a bank and eloping with her jailer date from this period between her two marriages. (She supposedly sent the guard back with a note sewn into his coat reading, "Returned because found unsatisfactory.") One account says she got away with $30,000. This is very unlikely. If it were true, she probably wouldn't have had to get involved in horse theft (ripping off a Cherokee named Andrew Pleasant Crane), which she was charged with in July of 1882.

By this time, Belle had married Sam Starr, the three-quarter Cherokee son of the notorious Tom Starr. He was described as handsome, with long black hair that he wore under a broad-brimmed hat. She was likely thirty-two, though the marriage license says twenty-seven. Sam Starr (charged with her for the horse theft) was just twenty-three. They settled in Arkansas.

The young couple appeared before "Hanging Judge" Isaac C. Parker (who makes more than one appearance on these pages) in March of 1883 at Fort Smith, Arkansas. Belle was convicted of both counts and Sam of one. They each got twelve-month sentences, to be served at the House of Correction in Detroit, but they served only nine months.

The Starrs' defense was that it was a case of mistaken identity, and that they'd been tending to old Tom Starr at the time of the thefts. It was quite a novelty for a woman to be charged with horse theft at that time, and the newspapers covered the trial heavily. *The Fort Smith* [Arkansas] *New Era* reported that Belle was a proficient rider and marksman. It added, "While she could not be considered even a good-looking woman, her appearance is of a kind as would be sure to attract the attention of wild and desperate characters." True enough.

Starr with Blue Duck, who killed a farmer for no apparent reason, in 1886. She believed in giving succor to outlaws, and tried to get Duck out on appeal. (Everett Collection Historical/Alamy Stock Photo)

Pearl Reed, aka Pearl Younger and Pearl Starr. She clashed with her mother. (Wikipedia)

Sam Starr was Reed all over again and was soon away from home despoiling the community most of the time. Meanwhile, Belle Starr was gaining a reputation for harboring fugitives from the law. In 1885 she was accused, with her husband and (maybe more than a friend) John Middleton, of stealing from the Seminole and Creek Indian treasuries.

Middleton ended up dead while trying to flee across a river. Belle Starr was arrested for the aforementioned larcenies in January of 1886. Instead of lying low, she was accused of robbing some farm settlements, dressed as a man. After pleading not guilty to those charges, she had a notorious photo of herself taken with convicted murderer Blue Duck (in shackles at the time). Duck's sentence was later reduced to life imprisonment.

Meanwhile, Sam and associates were charged with robbing the U.S. Mail, and they went into hiding. Belle was acquitted of the farm robberies, because no one could identify her as being present. She had again claimed to be elsewhere, in this case at a dance. She also got off on the horse theft charges.

Sam, after being shot off his horse and wounded by Indian police, turned himself in on October 4, 1886. He was released on bail, and it was only a few months later that— at a Christmas party on December 17, 1886 also attended by Belle—he was shot dead by rival Frank West (who also died in the encounter).

A CROOKED TRAIL WITH A BAD END

Given two chances to give up a life of crime, Belle Starr chose otherwise. With Sam Starr dead, she needed a new partner in crime. She found one in a young Creek Indian and Starr associate named Billy July (aka Jim Starr). The twenty-four-year-old was her third and last husband and, predictably, he was soon arrested and charged with horse theft. Belle's son, Eddie, then a teenager, was also charged with the same crime in July 1888. It ran in the family.

Around this time, showing rare good judgment, Belle attempted to back out of a deal to rent land to Edgar A. Watson, who was wanted for murder in Florida. They quarreled. She made the fatal error of telling Watson that the authorities in the Sunshine State might be interested in his whereabouts.

The movie version of Belle Starr bore no relation to reality.

On February 2, 1889, Belle and her young husband set out from their home at Younger's Bend in Oklahoma. July was going to his horse theft hearing, and Belle was headed out for a day of shopping. The next day, she started back without July and stopped at a house belonging to the Rowes, who frequently entertained on Sundays. Watson was there.

Belle, nibbling cornbread, headed back to Younger's Bend, but was hit with a shotgun blast near the Watson home. The horse made it home, but Belle did not.

The newspapers described the shooting as a "cowardly act," and reported she'd been ambushed from dense chaparral by one concealed man, or possibly two, as she was about to ford a river. "The murderer is still at large," the paper said.

BELLE STARR IN THE POLICE PAGES

The legend of Belle Starr was built in the pages of the *National Police Gazette*, which had a hand in creating our shared folklore. In his 1941 book *Belle Starr, The Bandit Queen*, Burton Rascoe has a lot to say about this weekly purple pulp phenomenon. "*The National Police Gazette* was read presumably by the male half of the population only, and was to be found in bordellos, saloons, gambling houses, pool halls, livery stables and barber-shops," Rascoe wrote. "Nonetheless, it crystallized and sustained a national code of morals and honor. It provided a way of thinking, a pattern of conduct, a point of view and a rationale of sentiment that were adopted by at least 90 percent of the male population of the United States—and, by a sort of spiritual contagion, 90 percent of the female contingent, also."

Rascoe said the *Gazette* had the hearty support of brewers, distillers, and saloon keepers, because it pushed the message that it was "immoral, degrading and ungentlemanly to drink alone, whether at a bar or in the privacy of one's home." Other messages include that it is cowardly to shoot your foe in the back or face to face, unless he has made a move on his gun or knife first; and it is your duty to knock a man down if he says something stronger than "shucks" in the presence of a lady; and a man who cheats at cards "deserves to be shot down like a dog." Oh, and never hit a man wearing glasses, and no spitting tobacco juice across a lady's path.

The *Gazette*'s most colorful editor, Dublin-born Richard K. Fox, was a boxing promoter and journalist who bought the paper in 1876 (only two years after arriving in America). Rascoe reports that the paper was caught flat-footed by Belle Starr's murder in 1889, and rushed into print a quickie twenty-five-cent book called *Bella Starr, the Bandit Queen, or the Female Jesse James*.

"This narrative does not have a single essential fact correct; her name and date of birth are both wrong in the Fox story, and from there on, the yarn is a masterpiece of a hack writer's invention," says Rascoe. "Unhampered by restricting facts, and inspired by having a female bandit to write about, the anonymous Fox Publications genius really went to town."

The Belle (or "Bella") Starr you got for a quarter was a great beauty, an ace horsewoman and crack shot, well educated, a gifted writer, a talented musician, and more amorous than Cleopatra. It's amazing that through that fog of early obfuscation, we can get a glimpse of the real Belle Starr. It isn't really all that romantic a story.

Opposite: Belle Starr as fancifully depicted and glamorized in the pages of the Police Gazette. *(Wikipedia)*

Watson, accused of the crime by both Belle's husband and her son, was in fact arrested for it, but without any real evidence, he was acquitted. The trail goes cold after that. July could have arranged the murder himself, since he was reportedly having an affair. But he was gunned down by a deputy only weeks after Belle died. Daughter Pearl had many conflicts with her mother, but her involvement is unlikely. Tom Starr's name is occasionally brought up as a suspect, in revenge for turning her son toward crime, but since it was the family business, this seems far-fetched.

A twist is provided by a letter from Vada McBride, a Californian who wrote to *Frontier Times* magazine in 1969. It was McBride's mother-in-law, Elmorah McBride, who made the cornbread that Belle—who "talked rough and cursed a lot"—was munching when she was shot. Elmorah claimed it was a neighbor, one James Ivy, who gunned Belle down, allegedly because he didn't want her talking about some skullduggery he was involved in. When asked why she didn't report what she knew, McBride said that no one crossed "Old Man Ivy" and lived to tell about it. Ivy doesn't come up in other discussions of who might have killed Belle Starr.

Meanwhile, Watson, who many think was the guilty party, went back to Florida and was gunned down by a posse there. So, even if no one was convicted of the crime, the most likely suspects were, in any case, soon dead.

Later on, in the spring of 1933, when Belle Starr's name was famed throughout the land, a woman named Flossie appeared and claimed to be Starr's long-lost granddaughter, given away by daughter Pearl to gypsies and raised in an orphanage. Her tale is in the *Dallas Morning News*. According to Flossie, Pearl's brother, Eddie—jealous of Belle's attention to Pearl—was the real killer.

WHERE THEY WENT BAD

Belle should never have become Mrs. James Reed, Mrs. Sam Starr, and Mrs. Billy July. Weren't there any nice boys in Carthage? And had Jim Reed actually started a new life in California, instead of reverting to type, she might have settled down and we would never have heard of Belle Starr. She seemed happy out there. But Belle was attracted to the dangerous types and went along with their criminal schemes—she may have even initiated some of them.

WHAT THEY SAID

Belle told the *Dallas Morning News*, in 1886, "I am a friend to any brave and gallant outlaw." Belle wrote in a letter that she was at last hoping to lead a quiet life on sixty acres at Younger's Bend, on the South Canadian River in Oklahoma. "I have become estranged from the company of women (whom I thoroughly detest) so I selected a place that few have had the gratification of gossiping around." It didn't work. "It soon became noised around that I was a person of some notoriety from Texas, and from that time on, my home and actions have been severely criticized."

Starr also claimed to have been visited at Younger's Bend by Jesse James himself. "Jesse James first came in and remained several weeks," she wrote. "He was unknown to my husband, and he never knew til long afterwards that our home had been graced by James' presence. I introduced him as one Mr. Williams from Texas."

HOODOO BROWN

(1856-1910)

BAD HAT WITH A STAR

APPALL-O-METER: 8

HOODOO BROWN

THE LEGEND

Hoodoo Brown—a small-time western Boss Tweed who used the levers of power to further his criminal enterprises—was the epitome of a lawman gone wrong. His case shows the fluidity of the lawman and badman divide at that time. Remember, John Wesley Hardin practiced law *after* he murdered dozens of people, and many a gunslinger became town marshal. People evidently like Brown's story, because characters named Hoodoo Brown appear in modern video games, comic books, and novels. A barbecue restaurant in Ridgefield, Connecticut, also bears his name.

HOW THEY GET IT WRONG

They get it wrong by confusing this Hoodoo Brown, born Hyman G. Neill, with another one, George W. (Hoodoo) Brown. They were both colorful. George Brown fought for the North in the Civil War, shot it out with Indians in the Dakotas, served as an army scout, and was a pioneer in building Dodge City, Kansas. Although he had a reputation as a gunman and was arrested for the murder of one "Crazy" Burns, he was acquitted and stayed on the right side of the law. George Brown's photo is sometimes used to illustrate stories about the *other* Hoodoo Brown, who used the law solely as a means to an end.

WHAT WE ACTUALLY KNOW

The man who became the notorious Hoodoo Brown was born Hyman G. Neill in Lexington, Missouri, to a prominent family with roots in Lee County, Virginia. His father, a lawyer named Henry Neill, was an upstanding citizen whose father fought in the War of 1812 and his grandfather in the Revolution. The family relocated from Virginia in the 1830s. Henry Neill fought in the Civil War on the Union side, attaining the rank of major, though he had Confederate sympathies.

The teenage Hyman (not yet Hoodoo) was a restless sort and left home early. Telling his bosses on the *Standard Herald* newspaper in Warrensburg, Missouri, he was "going to get your durn rags" (to make into newsprint), he hopped a freight train instead.

Although he worked as a buffalo hunter, hauled timber, toiled in silver mines, and ran an opera company in Mexico, he also went bad early as a con artist and gambler. George "Hoodoo" Brown looked like a businessman, but Hyman was described as tall, thin, and mustachioed, with a "rakish look." In a fuzzy unprintable photo, he is the epitome of the western outlaw.

Las Vegas, New Mexico during Hoodoo Brown's reign. (City of Las Vegas Museum and Rough Rider Memorial Collection)

VIVA LAS VEGAS

Hoodoo Brown washed up in Las Vegas, New Mexico, which even before he got there had a reputation as being wide open for crime. Bad hombres flocked there, and by 1879, they had enough voters to get Hoodoo Brown elected as Justice of the Peace. He also served as coroner (very convenient) and mayor.

The town was run by an incredible rogues' gallery, which became known as the Dodge City Gang. Hoodoo Brown was the ringleader, but there was also "Dirty" Dave Rudabaugh and Mysterious Dave Mather. Both became town officials in Las Vegas.

Rudabaugh (who possibly got his nickname because he never bathed) was a cattle rustler and holdup man who took on stagecoaches and trains in the 1870s and 1880s

before he was signed on to the coroner's jury in Las Vegas. Connecticut native Mather was reportedly a descendant of Cotton Mather; he became constable, was also a train robber, murderer, and rustler who rode (and got arrested) with the notorious Dutch Henry. Later, this survivor of a knife fight in Dodge City became both deputy sheriff and deputy city marshal of that town. Also, in Dodge City, he feuded with bar owner Thomas Nixon and delivered four bullets to the man's back. By 1878, he was in Mobeetie, Texas, selling fake gold bars.

"Mysterious" Dave Mather was another card-carrying member of the Dodge City Gang. His past included surviving a Dodge City knife fight, and selling fake gold bars in Texas. Wyatt Earp was rumored to have been a partner on some of his misadventures. (Wikipedia)

Another sometime member of the gang was Joshua Webb, who worked both sides—this town marshal reportedly owned a saloon with Doc Holiday and rode with Bat Masterson. Later, in 1880, he was arrested for murder. To give a sense of what Las Vegas, New Mexico, was like in those days, here's what the *Boston Globe* had to say in 1883:

> Hoodoo was made Marshal to keep him out of deviltry and make his talent for getting the drop of some use, but he just took advantage of it by standing up strangers on dark nights and cleaning 'em out. The justice of the peace was in cahoots with him [actually, Brown *was* justice of the peace] and a pretty pair of birds they were to run a town.

In the same story, a tale is told of a saloon patron getting "drunker'n Billy Bedlam" on "bug juice" and "blazing away" with his six-shooter at the roof. Brown reached behind his back and shot him between the eyes, reportedly without even turning around. The locally based writer concludes, "I ain't in favor of Hoodoo as a general proposition, but I give him credit for making a sensible man out of one blamed idiot with a pistol."

This kind of "law and order" wasn't built to last, but it endured for two years, during which the Dodge City Gang robbed stage coaches and trains, stole cattle, and were held responsible for several lynchings and murders. By 1880, the gang had the town fed up.

Opposite: "Dirty" Dave Rudabaugh (so named because he never bathed) was a member of the Dodge City Gang with Hoodoo Brown, "Mysterious" Dave Mather and Joe Carson. (Wikipedia)

One particularly shocking murder was that of a freighter named Mike Kelliher. He was ambushed by Neill and the gang, shot dead, and relieved of $1,900.

At one point, Dave Rudabaugh declared he was going to start living "on the square," but in reality, he continued raising hell. Rudabaugh had at one time been arrested by Webb, but let bygones be bygones and attempted to free the man after he was arrested for murder. In the fracas a jailer named Antonio Lino was shot dead.

After being incarcerated with Webb, the pair plotted a breakout. They first tried to shoot their way out, killing another jailer, Thomas Duffy. That didn't work, but they were successful with three other breakouts in the fall of 1881, escaping by digging through the walls. Rudabaugh continued rustling, relocated to Mexico, and was beheaded there in 1886. Webb ended his days as a railroad man.

Hoodoo Brown didn't fare all that well, either. In the summer of 1880, a posse of outraged citizens formed and drove him out of town. Reportedly, he stole some money from a dead man on his way out of town, heading for Houston. The local paper wrote admiringly that many noted criminals figured out how to break out of jail, but not many were smart enough to avoid their old haunts.

Escaping to Houston didn't help, however, because Brown was arrested there and charged with murder and robbery. While in jail in Texas, he reportedly had an amorous encounter with the widow of one of his deputies. According to the *Parsons Sun*, quoted in Erin Turner's *Outlaw Tales of the Old West*, "The meeting between the pair is said to have been affecting in the extreme, and rather more affectionate than would be expected under the circumstances."

Amazingly enough, Brown's gambit of hiring a pair of attorneys to defend him was successful, and they got him sprung. The local word was that he took off with the widow. *The Chicago Times*, also quoted by Turner, reported that since his release he and the widow were seen "skylarking through some of the interior towns of Kansas."

The details of Brown's demise are unclear, but he reportedly passed on in Coahuila, Mexico, leaving a common-law wife and son. He was buried back in Lexington as Henry G. Neill. The grave stone says the end came in 1910.

Opposite: The Old Town in Las Vegas, New Mexico. (Asaavedra32/Wikipedia)

Sometime later, a woman named Elizabeth Brown—reportedly a heavy drinker—turned up in Leadville, Colorado, claiming to have been married to Hoodoo. She says he was shot dead in a gambling dispute. A newspaper account from 1880 does indeed have Hoodoo shooting it out with another gambler, Charley Frank, across a table in Buena Vista, Colorado. "Brown is dead, and Frank cannot survive," it said. But Hoodoo may have lived much longer.

REMEMBERING HOODOO BROWN

Las Vegas, known today for its Hispanic food, has a historical museum that may be worth visiting. But don't expect a grand retrospective of all things Hoodoo Brown. The 2019 Heritage Week gave him a miss. A *New York Times* travel story from 2007 mentions that Billy the Kid hung out in Las Vegas, Doc Holiday had a dentist's office, and Teddy Roosevelt recruited for the Rough Riders there, but it doesn't mention Hoodoo Brown, once a leading citizen.

Las Vegas today still looks the part of an Old West town. It's been used as a film set, including for *Easy Rider*, *Wyatt Earp*, and *No Country for Old Men*.

WHERE THEY WENT BAD

There doesn't appear to have been a fork in the road for Hoodoo Brown. He went bad as soon as he hopped a freight train out of Missouri, evidently having decided that the straight life of work as a printer's devil was for squares.

WHAT THEY SAID

No actual dialogue from Neill/Brown survives, but the *Parsons Eclipse* reported on the arrest in Houston: "The offense committed at Las Vegas, as near as we can gather the facts relating to it, was murder and robbery, and the circumstances connected with the arrest here would indicate that the lesser crime of seduction and adultery was connected with it."

JOHNNY RINGO

(1850-1882)

A GUNMAN WHO DIED MYSTERIOUSLY

APPALL-O-METER: 5

JOHNNY RINGO

THE LEGEND

He may not be as famous as Bat Masterson, Wyatt Earp, or Doc Holiday, but this Shakespeare-quoting outlaw was associated with all three of them. Johnny Ringo left an enigmatic tale that has been fodder for popular entertainment since his disputed death in 1882.

HOW THEY GET IT WRONG

You probably think you know the story of Johnny Ringo from Lorne Greene's massive 1964 hit "Ringo," which topped the charts for six weeks. Although the story of a murderous outlaw who turns good at the end bears no actual resemblance to Johnny Ringo's life, Greene himself thought it was about the real-life fellow.

Further distortions can be found in numerous movies and TV shows, including *The Gunfighter, City of Bad Men, The Johnny Ringo Story, Gunfight at the O.K. Corral*, and *Doc*, to name a few. A TV series called *Johnny Ringo* ran for one season (1959-1960) and starred Don Durant in the title role, and it even spawned a Dell comic book. "Johnny uses outlaw bait to trap a lawless gang!" Wait a minute, he was lawless himself!

In truth Johnny Ringo (like Calamity Jane) just had a cool name—even though it was his real one. Hollywood felt free to expropriate that name for its own ends.

Johnny Ringo in 1880. (Wikipedia)

WHAT WE ACTUALLY KNOW

Like many Western legends, Johnny Ringo (born John Peters Ringo) got his start in the East. He was born on May 3, 1850, in Wayne County, Indiana. The town was Washington then, but now it's Green's Fork. Ringo's parents were Martin and Mary Peters Ringo, and they had four other children, three of them girls.

When Johnny was seven, they moved west to Gallatin, Missouri, where the girls were born, and then followed the American herd west again—headed for a new start in California, where Mary's sister lived. Along the way, Martin Ringo somehow shot himself to death with his own shotgun. Despite that tragedy, the family completed the arduous journey to San Jose, California.

Some reports say that young Ringo was a juvenile delinquent and prodigious drinker, but that was reportedly based on uninformed information from a distant relative and can't be proven. In the 1870 census, he's a farmer—as were the vast number of Americans at the time. It was shortly after that census that Ringo set off on his own, initially to see relatives in Indiana. By 1874, he was in Texas and had his first brush with the law—Ringo was arrested for shooting off his pistol in public in the town of Burnet.

THIS RINGO HAD A HEART

Lorne Greene's song "Ringo" is a frontier character study of an outlaw who was the fastest gun in the west. His life is saved by the lawman narrator, but then he goes on to "spread terror near and far."

But then the moment comes when the posse the narrator is riding with tracks Ringo down, and the lawman goes in to face the man alone. Ringo, in a lightning fast move, shoots the gun out of his hand, but then fails to administer the *coup de grace*:

> The gun went flying from my fist
> And I was looking down the bore
> Of the deadly .44 of Ringo
> They say that was the only time
> That anyone had seen him smile
> He slowly lowered his gun and then he said to me 'We're even, friend.'
> And so at last I understood
> That there was still a spark of good in Ringo.

A minute later, "a dozen guns spit fire and lead" and Ringo falls. The story is spread that the lawman beat Ringo to the draw, but one man knows different—and he puts his guns away.

The real Ringo doesn't appear to have shown such charity. Whenever he got the drop on someone, they got dead—or, like Louis Hancock—they got lucky.

A DIFFICULT CHARACTER

Ringo's future friend from Tombstone, Billy Breckenridge, was quoted in a 2005 *True West* article that Ringo was "a mysterious man. He had a college education, but was reserved and morose. He drank heavily as if to drown his troubles; he was a perfect gentleman when sober, but inclined to be quarrelsome when drinking. He was a good shot, and afraid of nothing." There's no proof one way or the other about the college education, but there's no direct evidence of it.

Ringo was in the right place at the right time to be involved in the Mason County War, sometimes referred to as the Hoodoo War, of 1875, one of many historical incidents that offers proof—if any were needed—that race relations on the frontier were less than harmonious.

The dispute was between German and American-born settlers, and it began with charges of stolen cattle. TexasHillCountry.com reports in the 2016 "The Hoodoo War of Mason County" article:

> It was common practice for stockmen to herd stray cattle when driving cattle for sale. Cattlemen seemed to have an understanding that 'if you brand some of my calves, I'll brand some of yours.' However, the German settlers did not agree with this practice. They maintained small herds, and the loss of one calf meant the loss of much-needed money. Adding to the tension was a group of wanderers that came to Texas after the Civil War ended. These men were outlaws through and through, and seemed to especially focus on cattle rustling.

Events exploded in May of 1875 when an American man named Tim Williamson was murdered by a mob while being escorted to the town of Mason by Deputy Sheriff John Wohrle. Not only did Wohrle fail to aid Williamson, he shot his horse so he couldn't get to safety.

METRO-GOLDWYN-MAYER
presents

RINGO AND HIS GOLDEN PISTOL

starring

MARK DAMON
VALERIA FABRIZI

in **EASTMANCOLOR**

Franco DE ROSA / **Giulia RUBINI** / **Loris LODDI** / **Andrea AURELI** / **Pippo STARNAZZA** and **ETTORE MANNI**

Subject and screenplay by A. Bolzoni · F. Rossetti
Directed by Sergio Corbucci · Produced by Joseph Fryd
A Sanson Film Production

The Johnny Ringo legend lives on. (Everett Collection, Inc./Alamy Stock Photo)

Williamson's good friend, Scott Cooley, an ex-Texas Ranger was so angered by this—and by the lack of indictments for the mob murder—that he shot Wohrle dead. Things escalated when Ringo's friends Moses Baird and George Gladden were ambushed and murdered. Ringo was part of a posse that tracked down and shot the man responsible for the ambush, James Chaney (also written Cheyney), in the presence of his family, some accounts add.

Ringo was arrested for threatening the life of the Burnet County Sheriff and his deputy. He was convicted, but later won an appeal. The case took a long time to come to court, and meanwhile, in May 1876, Ringo and his friend Scott Cooley were sprung from jail. During one of his stints in jail, Ringo allegedly met and befriended the notorious John Wesley Hardin.

The original charge of threatening the sheriff was overturned on appeal, but now Ringo was charged with murdering Chaney. Attorneys were good in those days, and Ringo's got him released on a $2,500 bond. He was promptly arrested again for disturbing the peace. Again, Ringo was lucky with the law—the murder case was dismissed because nobody wanted to testify against him.

After all this, he got himself elected constable at Loyal Valley, Texas, but it's unclear if he actually took up the post. He then moved on to Tombstone Territory, Arizona. According to JohnnyRingo.com, he "blended in quickly with the often-rowdy and violent rural cowboy element." Around this time, he was also identified as "John Ringgold," and that false identification (possibly arising from translations in German newspapers) confuses the historical record.

The *Arizona Daily Star* describes Ringo getting into a beef with one Louis Hancock. Ringo wanted Hancock to drink whiskey, but Hancock preferred beer. For this, Ringo hit Hancock on the head with his pistol then shot the man—who barely survived.

With the legendary Ike Clanton, Ringo (who appears to have skipped town to avoid the Hancock trial) is next seen in 1880 in New Mexico, where he helps drive some cattle to the San Carlos Indian Reservation. A few months later, he was listed as an election judge in San Simon, Arizona. Once again, it defies belief that a man with such a checkered past could be elected to a responsible position.

In Austin, Texas, in 1881, Ringo decided that three men sitting in a hallway had taken his misplaced money and he held them at gunpoint and searched them for the cash. Again, Ringo was arrested on a disturbing the peace charge and for carrying a pistol. The fine was $25.

A FEW MORE CRIMES

August 1881 Ringo and an accomplice held up a poker game and took $500.

January 1882 Ringo confronted Wyatt Earp and Doc Holiday, apparently believing they were spreading rumors about his involvement in a stage robbery. It could have escalated into a gun fight (if so, history would be different), and guns were waved, but cooler heads intervened before that point. Holiday and Ringo got $30 fines. Earp, a deputy U.S. marshal, had the right to carry a gun and so wasn't fined.

The hostilities between the men continued. When Ringo (in jail for robbery) heard that Wyatt Earp was planning to arrest his friend Ike Clanton, he managed to maneuver a release on bond through his attorney and rode out to warn Clanton. Once again, a confrontation loomed but was defused, in part by Clanton, who arranged for Ringo to stand down.

March 1882 Ringo was suspected in the shooting death of Morgan Earp, but history has absolved him of the crime. He had also earlier been accused of involvement in the shooting of Virgil Earp, but there's no evidence of that, either. Ringo was also let go on the robbery charge. Once again, there were no witnesses.

Ringo, despite living an apparently charmed life up to this point, didn't have long to live. He missed the Gunfight at the O.K. Corral—he was in California visiting his sisters—but soon returned to Arizona, no doubt blaming the Earps and Doc Holiday for the bloodshed.

The grave site of Johnny Ringo. Did he commit suicide, or was he murdered? (Wikipedia)

VISITING RINGO

Johnny Ringo was buried in Cochise County, Arizona. There's a Johnny Ringo State Historical Landmark on East Turkey Creek Road. *True West* reports that Ringo "most likely committed suicide, while on a bender, near a large oak tree in West Turkey Creek." The site that contains the rough-hewn stone is on private land, but visitors can ask to get permission to follow the trail to the site. Warren Baxter Earp, the youngest of the Earp brothers and one of Ringo's enemies in life, sleeps peacefully near him today in the Pioneer Cemetery.

A SAD END

By July of 1882, he was back in Tombstone and—a problem all his life—drinking heavily. He left town on July 11 and was seen taking a meal at Dial's Ranch. Witnesses said he was consistently inebriated. Ringo was found dead sitting against a tree on July 14, a gunshot wound in his right temple and a .45 caliber Colt in his right hand. He had been dead for at least twenty-four hours.

This death has become hugely controversial, and whole books have been written about what may have happened. Oddities abounded. Ringo's boots were off and his cartridge belt on upside down. Some said his gun had not been fired, and that a powder burn—expected in suicide at close range—was missing. There was talk about Ringo's Stetson hat—why was it still on his head? But evidence suggests it was found near his body. Wyatt Earp has also been implicated in the killing.

Ringo was known to be depressed at the time of his death. "All the evidence points to suicide," says JohnnyRingo.com, and that conclusion is supported in two biographical books, *John Ringo: The Gunfighter Who Never Was* and *John Ringo: King of the Cowboys*.

WHERE THEY WENT BAD

Heavy drinking, perhaps from a relatively young age, and a lack of impulse control, particularly when under the influence, contributed to Ringo taking the wrong path.

WHAT THEY SAID

Ringo explained in a letter why he could not appear to address the charges of shooting Louis Hancock on December 9, 1879. He said, "I got shot through the foot and it is impossible for me to travel for a while. If you get any papers for me, and will let me know I will attend to them at once. As I wish to live here, I do not wish to put you to any unnecessary trouble, nor do I wish to bring extra trouble on myself."

Attributed to either Ringo or his accomplice Bill Williams in a Texas Rangers report: The men said they had "made beef of Cheyney and if someone did not bury him he would stink."

THE RUFUS BUCK GANG

(ALL EXECUTED 1896)

MULTI-RACIAL RAMPAGE

APPALL-O-METER: 9

THE RUFUS BUCK GANG

THE LEGEND

Similarities abound between the crimes of the Rufus Buck Gang and Cherokee Bill's mob. Both groups of outlaws were non-white actors in a racist society that undoubtedly stymied opportunities for legitimate advancement. But their crimes are so horrific, and so random—and include African-American, Native American, and Hispanic victims— that blaming society (even an unjust one) seems a stretch.

It has been said that Buck's aim was to trigger a Native uprising that would end up with the territory reclaimed and the white invaders expelled, but the actual crimes speak against anything but criminal opportunism.

HOW THEY GET IT WRONG

Not much has been written about the Rufus Buck Gang, so misinformation is not a major issue. There is a sin of omission, perhaps, in ignoring a particularly bloody incident. But these were violent times.

The Rufus Buck Gang was integrated. Rufus is at center with (from left) Maomi July, Sam Sampson, Luckey Davis and Lewis Davis. (Wikipedia)

WHAT WE ACTUALLY KNOW

The crimes of the Rufus Buck Gang occurred in Indian Territory (Arkansas and Oklahoma) during a very unsettled period in American history, 1895 to 1896. The territory was still recovering from the Civil War and dealing with the outcomes and atrocities from the horrific Trail of Tears, which forced the Creek, Cherokee, Seminole, Chickasaw, and Choctaw tribes to march thousands of miles from their ancestral homes.

Rufus Buck, only eighteen at the time and of mixed Creek and African-American parentage, was the leader, and his teenage crew included Sam Sampson and Maoma July (both Creeks) and brothers Lewis and Lucky (or Luckey) Davis. All of them had records for minor offenses and had served time in the Fort Smith jail.

Their murderous spree began in July of 1895, with Buck allegedly boasting, according to a National Park Service report, "that his outfit would make a record that would sweep all the other gangs of the territory into insignificance." They made good on that pledge, though it perhaps did not gain them the historical notoriety they sought.

SCENE OF THE CRIME

Fort Smith, where the Rufus Buck Gang was hanged on July 1, 1896, is a historic site today. The fort's historical page reads as follows:

> While the stories of the outlaws charged with violent crimes such as rape and murder are most commonly associated with this court, the majority of cases heard by Judge Parker were not capital crimes. Individuals were arrested and brought to the Fort Smith jail on charges such as petty theft, whiskey peddling, arson, illegal timber cutting, and violation of the postal laws.

PEOPLE RANDOMLY ATTACKED

There is only sketchy information on the Buck gang's many crimes, but some accounts survive. The first victim, say some sources, was Deputy Marshall John Garrett, shot near Okmulgee, Oklahoma, on July 28, 1895. They weren't done for the day, because after killing the lawman, the gang kidnapped and raped a woman named Mrs. Wilson—who was one of the few survivors of their onslaughts.

On July 31, the gang encountered a man and his daughter in a wagon. The man was held at gunpoint and the girl taken. It's unclear what fate they met. The gang was working themselves into a murderous frenzy.

Around the same time, an African-American boy (name not recorded) was murdered, and a man named Ben Callahan was beaten, possibly to death—the accounts aren't clear. The gang took his boots, saddle, and money.

A man named Gus Chambers was murdered when he tried to prevent the theft of his horses. On August 2, 1895, the gang robbed a stockman of everything he had, including his clothes, and shot at him as he fled naked. Two days after that, on August 4, they gang-raped Rosetta Hansen (or Hassan), holding her husband off with their rifles. Again, it's unclear if she died. Other women were also killed, including a Miss Ayres and an Indian girl. They robbed country stores at Orket, Oklahoma, and murdered two women and a fourteen-year-old girl. Creek and white settlements were equally attacked.

Finally, a mixed force of lawmen and Indian police of the Creek Light Horse caught up with the gang outside Muskogee, Oklahoma, on August 10. Hanging Judge Isaac Parker was again presiding, and he sentenced the five to death. An appeal to the U.S. Supreme Court was, not surprisingly, unavailing. The five were hanged on July 1, 1896 at Fort Smith.

In the absence of much historical data, some interpreters of this story have turned to fiction. Leonce Gaiter wrote *I Dreamt I was in Heaven: The Revenge of the Rufus Buck Gang*. Gaiter says he saw a clipping that contained the only known photo of "five young men of wildly varying shades of brown, circa 1895."

Gaiter wrote in a 2011 Rap Sheet blog post, "I was hooked. First the name 'Rufus Buck' was awesome. Such a name would practically predestine one for outlawry. The idea of men so young embarking on such a mad scheme suggested both near-religious zeal and childish naiveté—for me, an irresistible combination."

Harvard Magazine wrote in 2012, that Gaiter portrays the gang not as even faintly romantic, but as "lost, dimwitted, unloved souls staggering clumsily through the world, creating havoc not from evil plans but from sheer teenage impetuosity." A careless toss of a lantern by one gang member incinerates a barn then burns down half a small town. It is "a volatile, high-testosterone mix of young male energy with no meaningful channel (or future)."

(Wikipedia)

WHERE THEY WENT BAD

Life must have been difficult for the young men of the Indian Territory, especially those of mixed race, fully at home in no community. Educational and employment opportunities were likely to be few. Their path of petty crime quickly escalated into something much darker.

WHAT THEY SAID

After his death, a photograph of Rufus Buck's mother was found in his cell, and on its reverse was a poem he had apparently written.

Spelling and capitalization were creative, but this is the gist:

> I dreamt I was in heaven
> Among the angels fair;
> I'd near seen none so handsome, that twine in golden hair;
> They looked so neat and sang so sweet and played the golden harp.
> I wanted to pick an angel out
> And take her to my heart;
> But the moment I began to plea I thought of you my love.
> There was none I'd seen so beautiful
> On earth or heaven above.
> Good by my dear wife and mother
> All so my sisters.

My, dream. - 1896.

I, dremp'T, I, WAS, in, HeAven,
Among, THe, AngeLS, FAir;
i'd, hear, seen, none, So, HANdSome,
THAT, TWine, in, Golden, HAir;
THeY, LooKed, So, neAT, ANd, SANg, So, Swee
ANd, PLAY,d, THe, THe, Golden, HARP,
I, WAS, ABouT, To, PicK, An, AngeL, ouT,
ANd, TAKe, HeR, To, mY, HEART;
BuT, THe, momenT, I, BeGAn, To, PLEA,
I, THougHT, of, You, mY, LoVe,
THere, WAS, none, i'd, Seen, So, BEAuTiFuLL
On, eARTH, or, HeAven, ABove.
Good, By, M,y, Dear, Wife, aNd, MoTHer
also, MY, SiSTers

I, DaY, of, JULY,   Rufus, BucK
Tu, THe, Yeore   Youse, TruLey
   off
  1896

HOLY GHOST
FATHER SON

virTue &, resur, resur, rection

Rufus Buck's last testament was this poem, scrawled on the back of a photograph of his mother. (Wikipedia)

Remembering the Trail of Tears. An estimated 2,000 to 4,000 of 16,000 Cherokees died. (Cherokee Heritage Center/Wikipedia)

THE TRAIL OF TEARS

The Rufus Buck Gang was a product of the dislocation caused by the Trail of Tears. Congressional passage of the Indian Removal Act in 1830 required the tribes of the Southeast—Choctaws, Muscogee Creeks, Seminoles, and Chickasaws—to give up their Southeastern lands and be relocated west of the Mississippi.

The Cherokee were also included, in part, because of the signing of the Treaty of New Echota in 1835 by a small faction of the tribe. The move was bitterly opposed by the tribal majority. The Cherokee removals began in May of 1838, involving more than 16,000 tribal members.

The National Park Service, in a brief online history of the Trail of Tears takes up the story:

> The impact of the resulting Cherokee 'Trail of Tears' was devastating. More than a thousand Cherokee—particularly the old, the young, and the infirm—died during their trip west, hundreds more deserted from the detachments, and an unknown number (perhaps several thousand) perished from the consequences of the forced migration. The tragic relocation was completed by the end of March 1839, and resettlement of tribal members in Oklahoma began soon afterward. The Cherokee, in the years that followed, struggled to reassert themselves in the new, unfamiliar land.

It was in this context that the Rufus Buck Gang was formed, though it's difficult—from the limited historical record—to prove that the gang's crimes were specifically related to the tribe's horrific history. We know they got in trouble early, but not why.

OTHER OWLHOOTS AND UNSAVORY CHARACTERS

OTHER OWLHOOTS AND UNSAVORY CHARACTERS

This book could have been much longer. It was hard to end it, because colorful outlaws kept popping up, begging to be included. The folks in this chapter are not well remembered, but they were certainly very real to the people who ended up on the wrong end of their weaponry.

"Killing Jim" Miller was known as "Deacon Jim" because he didn't drink or swear. But a deacon, he wasn't. (Wikipedia)

JAMES "KILLIN' JIM" MILLER (1866-1909)

James Miller, originally from Arkansas, was charged with murdering his grandparents at age eight, for crying out loud. He went to live with his sister's family, but that ended violently, too—young Jim shot his brother-in-law, Jim Coop, with a shotgun. He wasn't convicted of either crime, and seemed to lead a charmed life, despite strong evidence against him.

Miller was known for his teetotaling ways and impeccable manners, and he was also nicknamed Deacon Jim. According to *True West*, in 1888, he married Sallie Clements, a cousin of John Wesley Hardin. He served as a deputy sheriff in Pecos, Texas, but was fired for stealing cattle. Amazingly enough, after *this* he became town marshal in Pecos, which he turned into an open town along the lines of Hoodoo Brown's Las Vegas, New Mexico.

Miller moved regularly between criminality and law enforcement. He was hired by Reeves County Sheriff Bud Frazer as a deputy, but a long-simmering feud between the two finally came to a head in 1894 with a gunfight that left Miller near death (saved by a plate in his coat—the man had all the luck). Again, Miller beat the rap, this time because a key witness was gunned down. Miller finally killed Frazer in 1896 by discharging both barrels of a shotgun into his head, but again escaped prosecution.

Next, Miller got hired as an assassin by the cattle barons. The victims were homesteaders and, in the case of James Jarrott, their lawyer. Miller claimed to have killed fifty-one people. Finally, in 1909, Miller gunned down former U.S. Marshal Gus Bobbitt with a double-barreled shotgun. It's ironic that when Miller finally faced justice, it came via a mob. He was taken out by a lynch mob and hanged from the rafters of a barn. His last words, according to History.net, were "Let 'er rip."

DAN BOGAN (1860-1889, MAYBE)

A cowboy with a hot temper, Dan Bogan was born in Alabama and relocated to Texas, Wyoming, and New Mexico. Bogan, a talented cowhand, was suspected of cattle theft by the legendary New Mexico Sheriff Pat Garrett, but Bogan—who claimed the cows were mavericks—threatened a lawsuit and won an $800 settlement from the county. Nevertheless, Bogan was indicted for the crime soon after, in 1885, and—resisting arrest—he got into a shootout with Garrett, but escaped.

Bogan had reportedly killed three men by 1886, one of them a dance hall proprietor whose crime was barring him entry. He also tried to murder Bill Calkin, the owner of a paper in Wyoming who had angered him with statements in print. He then ambushed and killed

Dan Bogan, a cowboy with a short fuse. And in the end he got away clean. (Wikipedia)

a nemesis, former Texas Ranger Charles S. Gunn, the constable of the Wyoming town where he was living.

Bogan was captured after his crime spree, but managed to escape custody—though he was wounded on his way out of town. He finally surrendered, and in September of 1887 was convicted of murder. He escaped using smuggled saw blades. A $1,000 reward was put on Bogan's head.

The murderer was never apprehended again, and rumors put him in South America (following the Butch Cassidy trail), raising a family on a Texas ranch, or living in New Mexico under an assumed name. *The Laramie Sentinel* reported in 1889 that Bogan had been gunned down in Mexico.

"Wild Bill" Longley. He was a Confederate die-hard and racist in the manner of Jesse James and John Wesley Hardin. (Wikipedia)

WILLIAM PRESTON "WILD BILL" LONGLEY (1851-1878)

A post-Civil War Confederate racist in the manner of Jesse James, Longley was raised in Texas and also learned to handle a gun there. He was known as "a fast draw." He reportedly carried a pair of .44-caliber Dance revolvers, and a shotgun if needed.

In 1866 Longley, at age sixteen, killed an African-American policeman who he said had insulted his father. He also killed two other newly freed slaves in Lexington, Texas. He gunned down another former slave, Green Evans, in 1868. Black people who only got a whipping from him counted themselves lucky. And according to the website Legends of America, "Longley picked many a fight with anyone he suspected of being a Yankee sympathizer or a carpetbagger."

Longley "had a notoriously short fuse," reports *The 10 Deadliest Wild West Gunfighters* blog. He was suspected of horse theft and actually lynched, but as the mob rode off, one member fired back at the hanging man. By chance, the bullet frayed the rope and it broke, saving what by all accounts was a fairly worthless life. By 1870, Longley joined up with his brother-in-law, John W. Wilson, to kill more African-Americans (a man and a woman).

On his way to Kansas, possibly because there was a $1,000 reward for his capture in Texas, Longley killed a trail boss, a reputed horse thief, and a soldier (who had insulted women from Texas). He was caught, tried, and jailed, but escaped, enlisted in the U.S. Cavalry, and twice deserted. After that it was back to Texas and where he killed more black men. He was arrested but released by Mason County Sheriff J.J. Finney—possibly because Finney was paid off by one of Longley's relatives.

In 1874 Longley was persuaded by his uncle, Caleb Longley, to kill a man named Wilson Anderson. Then, the next year, George Thomas and William "Lou" Shroyer were his victims. He began sharecropping for the Reverend William Lay, but they got into a dispute and Longley shot the Reverend to death while he was milking a cow. He was finally caught in DeSoto Parish, Louisiana, by Nacogdoches County Sheriff Milton Mast, and held over for murdering Anderson. The jury found him guilty on September 5, 1877, and he was sentenced to be hanged.

In jail, Longley compared himself to John Wesley Hardin, who killed more men but escaped the hangman's noose with a prison sentence. He was jaunty on the gallows in front of a crowd of 4,000 people, asking that a loose board be repaired, because he wouldn't want to fall and break his neck. His last words: "So long, everybody!" Reported the *Galveston Daily News*, "Two moans escaped the lips, the arms and feet were raised three times, and after hanging 11.5 minutes life was pronounced extinct."

Top: Tom "Black Jack" Ketchum before getting his neck stretched. (Wikipedia)

Bottom: Hole in the Wall Gang member "Black Jack" Ketchum keeps his date with a necktie party in 1901. (National Archives)

TOM "BLACK JACK" KETCHUM (1863-1901)

This onetime Hole in the Wall Gang member was born in Texas and headed out to New Mexico in 1890, possibly one step ahead of the law. He promptly joined up with his older brother, Sam, and together in 1892 they robbed an Atchison, Topeka, and Santa Fe railroad train.

Ketchum was known to hole up at the Bassetts' Brown's Park, Colorado, ranch between jobs. Members of his gang included Butch Cassidy, associates Ben Kilpatrick, Harvey "Kid Curry" Logan, and his brother, Lonnie Curry. In 1895, Tom Ketchum was accused of taking part in the murder of his neighbor, John "Jap" Powers, in Tom Green County, Texas, and he later admitted his part in the crime (for money, apparently).

Ketchum was reportedly also involved in the kidnapping and murder of Albert Jennings Fountain and his son, Henry Fountain, in New Mexico in 1896. That same year, Ketchum and his mob robbed a store in Liberty, New Mexico, then managed to kill two members of the posse that came after them. Ketchum's next move, logically enough, was to join the Hole in the Wall Gang.

Sam Ketchum was wounded by a posse near Cimarron, New Mexico, was arrested, and died of his wounds in prison. Tom Ketchum kept to his old ways, singlehandedly attempting to rob a train on August 16, 1899. He was shot off his horse by conductor Frank Harrington, nursed back to health (minus his right arm), and convicted of "felonious assault upon a railroad train." He was supposedly the only person ever hanged in Union County, New Mexico. The hanging was botched, and Ketchum's head separated from his body. His last words: "Good-bye. Please dig my grave very deep. All right; hurry up."

BELLE SIDDONS, AKA MADAM VESTAL (1842–?)

Siddons, a child of privilege and reportedly a great beauty, was born in Jefferson City, Missouri, in 1842, part of a politically connected family from St. Louis. Siddon's uncle, Claiborne Fox Jackson, with whom she was close, was the fifteenth governor of Missouri. Belle attended the Missouri Female Seminary in Lexington, Missouri, and was a debutante and society queen. She used what she had. According to Donna Blake Birchell's *Wicked Women of New Mexico*, "Belle was considered to be a highly educated woman, so she knew how to use her intelligence and beauty to manipulate people." It's unfortunate that there do not appear to be any surviving photos of Belle.

Belle's family was Confederate through and through. A Confederate officer she gave her garter to, Captain Garret Lamb Parrish (some say the only man she ever loved), "became the devoted worshipper of the reigning belle," said the *San Francisco Examiner* in 1881. Alas, the dashing captain was gunned down in his first battle with the Union. "His death seems to have changed the entire disposition and course of life of Miss Siddons," the paper said.

Belle became a Confederate spy in St. Louis and would tease information from soldiers at DeBar's Opera House and feed it to Confederate Generals Sterling Price and Nathan Bedford Forrest. Unfortunately for her, the Union had spies, too, and her arrest was ordered by Union General Samuel Ryan Curtis—with whose men she had recently socialized. Belle had been warned by one of her many admirers, and she attempted to escape by the Southerners' "grapevine railway" but was caught in December of 1862, proudly admitted her guilt (challenging to court to shoot her "like the other spies"), and was sent to Grand Street Rebel Prison in St. Louis. She served only four months before being pardoned.

After the war, Belle landed on her feet, serving as a successful lobbyist in Jefferson City and again, according to the *San Francisco Examiner*, "became notorious for her subtle power and influence upon certain members of the legislature." There were rumors of all-night carousals, wine suppers, and mysterious excursions to St. Louis.

Siddon's life of crime started after she married Newt Hallett, a handsome surgeon. He was also a gambler, taught her cards, and moved her to Houston, Texas. There, she worked as Dr. Hallett's assistant, both in medicine and the popular game of faro. Things might have continued had not Hallett died in the 1869 yellow fever epidemic.

Belle briefly worked as a tutor to the Sioux tribe at the Red Cloud Agency, but when that didn't bring in enough money, she took off for New Orleans where she became a very successful card dealer, reinventing herself as "Madam Vestal."

The *Examiner* wrote:

> She never quarreled or exchanged words of anger. Her prompt argument was her pistol, which always lay beside her stacks of money. Her favorite costume was red or black velvet, ornamented with a profusion of gaudy jewelry, mostly diamonds and rubies. Her luxuriant black hair usually hung carelessly looped over her shoulders with gold and diamond clasps. This sensational costume, she said, was part of her stock in trade. 'It excites curiosity and draws in the suckers,' she said.

Madam Vestal became restless in the Big Easy, having heard of the big gold strikes out west. She subsequently dealt cards (including faro) in Wichita, Kansas, and Cheyenne, Wyoming. She didn't seem to get much pleasure out of taking those suckers. She remained impassive, win or lose, and admitted that she had never done a kind act, returned a dollar, or won or asked a favor since she became a gambler. She told the newspaper, "My luck was invariable, and I had a superstition that if I allowed the first thought of kindness to enter my soul it would break the spell. I hated every man who came to play against me; they came to break my bank. My husband never gave back money or spared either friend or foe in play; why should I?"

She then moved to Dakota Territory, where gold had been discovered in 1874. Belle was now calling herself Lurline Monteverde (or Monte Verde), but still wearing Madam's red dress. She hired a bunch of gamblers and "sporting girls" and in a caravan of wagons they headed over to Deadwood. The *Hat Creek Dateline* reported in August of 1876 that Ms. Monte Verde was "traveling in a yellow omnibus that has been remodeled into a comfortable home on wheels, with a bed, alcohol stove for light cooking, curtained windows and a shelf for books." At least a dozen of her dealers and bartenders were in other wagons, making a "colorful caravan."

Monteverde's Palace was soon open for business, and Lurline was the Queen of Deadwood. The local papers praised the queen as a "flawlessly groomed beauty, inviting, sultry and sensuous."

Belle's next partner was Archie McLaughlin, the former Archibald Cummings and a one-time member of Quantrill's Raiders. McLaughlin/ Cummings was a thoroughly bad guy, part of a well-organized gang of

Deadwood, South Dakota, as it was in 1876. Gold was discovered in the Black Hills in 1874. (National Archives)

stage robbers and road agents who bedeviled the coach routes between the Black Hills and the Union Pacific railroad for years. But Belle was madly in love and soon became his spy, gathering information on the movement of federal payrolls. She "became the confidante and adviser of the gang," the *Deadwood Daily Pioneer* wrote in 1924. "No

A BEAUTIFUL WRETCH.

The Sad Wreck of a Former Belle of the Frontier.

A Twenty Years' De cent from High Life to the Lowest.

Career of a Leadville Character.

San Francisco Examiner.

Siddons on the skids, as reported by the San Francisco Examiner.

robbery was undertaken of which she disapproved, and none failed in which she advised and planned the details."

McLaughlin was ambushed and wounded after getting bad information about a gold train, and he survived only because Belle (trained as a nurse by Dr. Hallett) ministered to him. The robber went back to robbing, but Belle was for once loose-lipped and gave information about her paramour's location to detective Boone May.

McLaughlin and his confederates were caught on a train bound for San Francisco and shipped to Cheyenne for trial, but on the way a mob ambushed the coach, grabbed the gang, and prepared to hang them en masse. Before he died, McLaughlin (who thought, wrongly, that he'd avoid the noose if he talked) gave up the location of the gang's stash. So now Belle (who survived a half-hearted suicide attempt after hearing of McLaughlin's death) was penniless and partner-less, as well as a drug addict and an alcoholic. "She lost all of her characteristic courage and surrendered herself to drink," the Deadwood newspaper wrote.

So great was her grief that Siddons became a wandering drunk. But after nearly being killed in a Deadwood avalanche, she pulled herself together enough by 1870 to relocate to Leadville, Colorado, and briefly operate the region's largest music hall. From there she drifted over to gang-controlled Las Vegas, New Mexico, (where she gambled at the Toe Jam Saloon). Belle had taken up with one Eugene Holman and may have had a daughter named Cora by him.

Belle could play the banjo and sing, and that's what she did at the Globe Theater in Las Vegas, and later at a brothel there named The Parlor. Around this time Belle (in the guise of Monte Holman) started sending poetry to the *Las Vegas Optic* newspaper, and one untitled verse from May 12, 1880, reads:

> Alas, my childhood and my blossoms faded,
> And I in stranger lands have wandered far.
> My buoyance is gone; I'm worn and jaded.
> And blighting sorrow came my joy to mar.

The final tragedy in Belle's life occurred after she persuaded a rich Las Vegas man to build a vaudeville theater for her, but it burned down in September 1880. A shell of what she once was, Belle wandered through Colorado and Arizona. From there, she next appeared as a resident of a San Francisco drunk tank, where the *San Francisco Examiner* encountered her in 1881.

The striking Belle Siddons was now wearing torn and dirty clothes, her hat and shawl having been torn off her when she resisted arrest. Her long hair hung over her face forming a veil. The *Bee* described her as "a pitiable object, a complete picture of abject misery and despair." But she was good for one more story. Not long after, according to Birchell's *Wicked Women of New Mexico*, she was found dead from an overdose in a San Francisco opium den. "This woman of such promise and social grace now rests in an unknown grave," Birchell concludes.

THE DALTON GANG

Top: Father James Lewis Dalton with sons Emmett and Robert, 1876. (RoughDiplomacy.com)

Bottom: Three of the Dalton brothers. (RoughDiplomacy.com)

This family of bank and train robbers is better known for how they died than how they lived. Lurid photographs (popular at the time) show four members of the gang, including two Daltons, either lying dead in a row or propped up, looking amazingly lifelike.

Just about everyone in the Old West appears to have met or been related to Cole Younger, and the Daltons were no exception. Their mother was Adeline Younger, who married Missouri bar owner Lewis Dalton, and was Cole's aunt. The five Dalton boys were Frank, Gratton ("Grat"), Bill, Bob, and Emmett, born between 1859 and 1871.

The oldest and "good" brother, Frank, became a Deputy U.S. Marshal, but he was gunned down in 1888. The four others went bad (including Bill, who joined the Wild Bunch), though they flirted with careers as posse members on the right side of the law. A dispute over not getting paid their wages sent them to the darker corners.

By 1890, Bob had been charged with smuggling whiskey into Indian Territory, and Grat with stealing horses. The gang, in addition to Bob, Emmett, and Grat, included Bill EcElhanie, George "Bitter Creek" Newcomb, Charley Pierce, and "Blackfaced" Charlie Bryant. Their first crime was taking out a gambling house in Silver City, New Mexico.

The brothers relocated to California where Bill was living a relatively legit life as a rancher, with a sideline in populist politics. In the latter role he had a beef with the Southern

Pacific Railroad's robber barons. Maybe that's why the gang decided to rob a Southern Pacific train heading to Los Angeles on February 6, 1891. It didn't go well. Bill, previously blameless, was now a murderer because they killed engineer George Radcliffe in the course of not getting away with any money.

Bob and Emmett evaded the posses, but Grat and Bill were apprehended. With Bryant and Newcomb, Bob and Emmett (now back in Indian Territory) ambushed a train and got away with $1,745. Grat, meanwhile, got a twenty-year sentence for the botched California robbery. He escaped, though, leaping out of a train window while in custody and landing unharmed in the San Joaquin River. Soon he was back with his brothers and robbing more trains.

Lest any reader form a sneaking admiration for this daring crime family, keep in mind that when they robbed a train in Adair, Oklahoma, in July 1892, stray shots hit and killed passenger W.L. Goff, a medical doctor. Another doctor was wounded.

By October 1892 the Dalton gang included Grat, Emmett, Bob, Bill Power, and Dick Broadwell. According to the Eyewitness to History blog, they rode into Coffeyville, Kansas, on the morning of October 5, with two of them in disguises that failed to prevent them from being recognized. The gang split up and walked into the town's two banks, Condon and Co. and First National. Powers, Broadwell, and Grat Dalton were assigned to the Condon; Bob and Emmett had the First National.

"The bank is being robbed!" yelled observer David Elliott, editor of the local paper. Inside the Condon, a trio of employees was ordered to fill a sack with money. But a crowd gathered, and townspeople took law into their hands and began firing into the bank. Reported Elliott

Bob (left) and Grat (right) Dalton. (RoughDiplomacy.com)

later, "The firing of the citizens through the windows became so terrific and the bullets whistled so close around their heads that the robbers and bankers retreated to the back room."

The same scene occurred at the First National. Bob and Emmett got their sack of money and then attempted to use the tellers as human shields so they could escape. But heavy fire made departure impossible.

The good citizens of Coffeyville got themselves armed to the teeth at Isham's Hardware Store. The store was also a good vantage point to cover the banks. Grat, Powers, and Broadwell didn't get more than twenty feet before they faced a storm of bullets. Grat and Powers were immediately shot dead. Broadwell made it to cover at the

The Dalton Gang, postmortem. From left, Bill Power, Bob Dalton, Grat Dalton and Dick Broadwell. (Dipper Historic/Alamy Stock Photo)

Long-Bell Lumber Company but was wounded in the back. He managed to get on his horse but was soon shot off it.

Meanwhile, Bob and Emmett Dalton got out of the First National and into a side alley. But they were within range of Isham's store, and fire from there. Emmett was wounded getting onto his horse, and was attempting to lift a similarly wounded Bob onto his horse and received both barrels of Carey Seamen's shotgun. The sack containing $20,000 fell into the street. Bob expired soon after, and that was the end of the Dalton gang.

Or was it? There is some speculation that an outlaw named Bill Doolin was along for the raid on Coffeyville. If so, he got away and continued to terrorize the populace of Kansas and Oklahoma for a few more years. He was gunned down in 1896 by Deputy U.S. Marshal Heck Thomas. He's buried in Guthrie, Oklahoma—right next to a onetime bank robber named Elmer McCurdy. According to a 2016 account in *True West* magazine, the latter achieved fame not in life (he was an inept bank robber) but after his 1911 death at the hands of law enforcement. McCurdy's body was embalmed and, when unclaimed by his family, exhibited around the country as "The Outlaw Who Would Never be Captured Alive."

McCurdy's corpse changed hands many times, and its owners eventually lost track of the fact it was an actual body, thinking it was instead a wax figure. In this form, it was featured in a traveling Museum of Crime. In 1976, during filming for an episode of The *Six Million Dollar Man*, the corpse's arm was accidentally broken off, revealing human bones and muscle tissue. A search revealed McCurdy's identity, and he finally got properly buried in 1977.

Emmett Dalton in prison. He was shot 23 times, but survived. (Wikipedia)

Though he was shot twenty-three times, Emmett Dalton somehow survived and was given a life sentence at the Kansas State Penitentiary. He served fourteen years and then became a Realtor and actor. Emmett also wrote the book *When the Daltons Rode*, which was published in 1931. The movie version came out in 1940. If you want to know more, visit the Dalton Museum in Coffeyville, which has mementos of the famous bank robbery, or the gang's secret hideout (with a ninety-five-foot tunnel) in Meade.

JEFFERSON RANDOLPH "SOAPY" SMITH II (1860-1898)

Smith is well-enough regarded that a commodious website (www.soapysmith.net) is dedicated to preserving his memory. He's better traveled than most of the outlaws profiled here, bilking people in Colorado, but also in Skagway, Alaska, operating from 1879 to 1898.

Of English descent, Smith's family had deep roots in old Virginia, but in 1821 moved to Coweta County, Georgia. In 1860, they went west and settled in Round Rock, Texas. Jefferson was on hand to see the legendary Texas outlaw Sam Bass get shot in 1878.

While still a teenager, he set out on his own as a confidence man and became adept at three-card Monte and shell games. More organized than most of his ilk, he formed the Soap Gang, pooled assets, and bribed politicians and lawmen. Saloon keepers got a cut for letting the gang prey on the customers.

A colorized image of Soapy Smith in his prime. (Soapysmith.net)

The Soap boys arrived in Denver, a wide-open town, in 1879. It was a haven for bunco gangs, and by 1884 Soapy Smith was on top of the heap. Among the now-gangster's associates were the "Reverend" John Bowers, who portrayed a man of the cloth, and "Professor" William Jackson, who claimed to be a mining expert. They had muscle, too, "Texas Jack" Vermillion and "Big Ed" Burns, among them.

Smith opened a few of his own gambling halls in Denver. "Caveat Emptor," said signs at the door. The establishments were veritable supermarkets of con, with fake mining offices, jewelry shops peddling paste, and auction houses offering nonfunctional watches. According to the Soapy Smith website, the Smith corridor was known as the "Streets of Doom," and if a traveler "could get from Union Station to Larimer Street without giving any money to members of the Soap Gang they would be relatively safe from financial harm."

Jefferson Randolph "Soapy" Smith bellies up the bar in Skagway. (Soapysmith.net)

Opposing Smith's enterprise were rival gangs and assorted reformers and do-gooders. There were at least two attempts to assassinate the king of the cons. Soapy finally fled town when his brother, Bascomb, was arrested on a charge of attempted murder. Soapy was also involved in that crime (though violence wasn't really his scene) but feared he'd get arrested as well. The Blonger brothers, Sam and Lou, took over the rackets in Denver.

By now it was 1896, and the Alaska Gold Rush was on. Soapy next turned up in the tent city of Skagway, just as it was being established. Again, he rose quickly through the ranks of bunco men, taking saloon owner John Clancy in as a partner. A popular scam was to take $5 from marks to send a telegram to their relatives. But there were no telegraph wires connecting Skagway then.

There was a good side to Soapy Smith—he took from the people but gave back to charitable institutions and took a genuine interest in the civic affairs of the towns he fleeced.

Top: Smith's gambling parlor in Skagway, Alaska. (Soapysmith.net)

After the battleship Maine was sunk in Havana, setting off the Spanish-American War, Smith saw his opportunity. He organized an all-volunteer militia named the Skaguay (the town's name then) Military Company and set himself up as captain. The governor and President of the United States were informed that the army was ready to serve. Taken seriously, Smith got permission to drill his troops at Fort St. Michael. Of course, the fort was 1,000 miles away, but Smith hung the proclamation in his saloon. They had a captured bald eagle as a mascot.

But public opposition was building over Soapy's cons, and vigilante groups formed. "Soapy Smith's Last Bluff Called by Frank Reid," read a headline in the *Skaguay News* for

July 15, 1898. What happened was this, Soapy got wind of a meeting of his antagonists at the wharf, and so he grabbed a Winchester rifle and headed there, trailed by his boys. Frank Reid, one of the vigilante guards, blocked Smith's path, and in the scuffle that followed both men were shot. Soapy was dead and Reid badly wounded. He latter succumbed.

Historians have argued about the incident, with some saying that it wasn't Reid who killed Smith but another one of the four guards, Jesse Murphy, who survived. In this telling, the deed was assigned to Reid, because if both antagonists were dead, there'd be no further bloodshed. It really doesn't matter all that much now, does it?

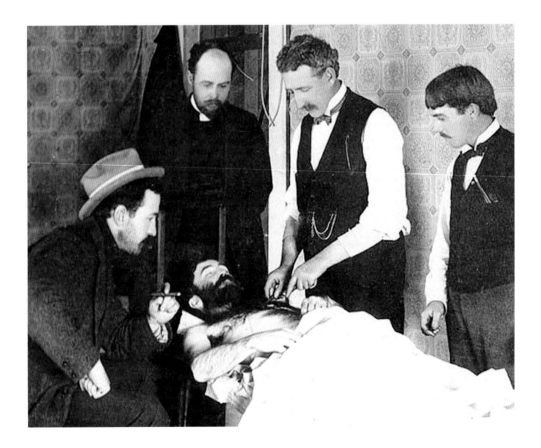

Soapy's autopsy. It's unclear who shot him. (Vital Archive/Alamy Stock Photo)

BIBLIOGRAPHY

Akins, Jerry, *Hangin' Times in Fort Smith: A History of Executions in Judge Parker's Court*, Butler Center for Arkansas Studies, 2012.

Birchell, Donna Blake, *Wicked Women of New Mexico*, The History Press, 2014.

Boren, Kerry Ross, *Butch Cassidy: The Untold Story*, Design Publishing, 2010.

Breihan, Carl, *Wild Women of the West*, Signet Books, 1982.

Burrows, Jack, *John Ringo: The Gunfighter Who Never Was*, University of Arizona Press, 1996.

Butts, Ed, *She Dared: True Stories of Heroines, Scoundrels, and Renegades*, Tundra Books, 2005.

Byrnes, Thomas, *1886 Professional Criminals of America*, Lyons Press, 2000.

Clavin, Tom, *Wild Bill: The True Story of the American Frontier's First Gunfighter*, St. Martin's Press, New York, 2019.

Durham, Philip, and Everett L. Jones, The Negro Cowboys, New York: Dodd, Mead & Company, 1965.

Edwards, John, *Noted Guerrillas: Warfare of the Border*, Bryan, Brand and Company, 1877.

Finkelstein, Norman, *The Capture of Black Bart: Gentleman Bandit of the Old West*, Chicago Review Press, 2018.

Froebel, Julius, *Seven Years' Travel in Central America, Northern Mexico, and the Far West of the United States*, Richard Bentley, 1859.

Gardner, Mark Lee, *To Hell on a Fast Horse: Billy the Kid, Pat Garrett, and the Epic Chase to Justice in the Old West*, William Morrow, 2010.

Garrett, Pat, *The Authentic Life of Billy the Kid*, Skyhorse, 2017.

Goldman, Stephen, *Wanted Dead or Alive: True Life Accounts of the Desperados of the Wild West*, Historical Briefs, Inc., 1994.

Gundel, Alex, *Charles Wells Banks' Extraordinary Journey through Life*, self published, 2019.

Hansen, Ron, *The Assassination of Jesse James by the Coward Robert Ford*, Harper Perennial (reprint edition), 2007.

Hardin, John Wesley, *The Life of John Wesley Hardin, As Written by Himself*, CreateSpace Independent Publishing Platform, 2014.

Hatch, Tom, *The Last Outlaws: The Lives and Legends of Butch Cassidy and the Sundance Kid*, NAL, 2013.

Jackson, Joseph Henry, *Bad Company: The Story of California Stage-Robbers, Bandits & Highwaymen*, Harcourt Brace, New York, NY, 1949.

James, Jesse, Jr., *Jesse James, My Father: The First and Only True Story of His Adventures Ever Written*, Charles River, 2018.

Katz, William Loren, *The Black West*, Revised Edition, New York: Broadway Books, 2005, first edition published 1971.

Lawless, Chuck, *The Old West Sourcebook: A Traveler's Guide*, Crown, 1994.

Love, Nat, *The Life and Adventures of Nat Love Better Known in the Cattle Country as Deadwood Dick by Himself*, University of Nebraska Press, 1995.

Michaelides, Marina, *Renegade Women of Canada: The Wild, Outrageous, Daring and Bold*, Great Canadian Stories, 2006.

Naden, Corrine and Rose Blue, *Belle Starr and the Wild West*, Blackbirch Press, 2000.

Nash, Jay Robert, *Encyclopedia of Western Lawmen and Outlaws*, De Capo Press, New York, NY, 1989.

Perkins, James E., *Tom Tobin Frontiersman*. Pueblo West, Colorado: Herodotus, 1999.

Price, Charles F., *Season of Terror: The Espinosas in Central Colorado, March-October 1863*, Timberline Books, 2013.

Raine, William MacLeod, *Famous Sheriffs and Western Outlaws: Incredible True Stories of Wild West Showdowns and Frontier Justice*, Skyhorse, 2012.

Rascoe, Burton, *Belle Starr: The Bandit Queen*, Random House, 1941.

Ravage, John W., Black Pioneers: Images of the Black Experience on the North American Frontier, University of Utah Press, 1998.

Rutter, Michael, *Wild Bunch Women*, Twodot, 2003.

Sante, Luc, *Low Life*, FSG, 1991.

Scott, Bob, *Tom Tobin and the Bloody Espinosas*, Publish America, 2004.

Siringo, Charles A., *History of Billy the Kid*, Kessinger Publishing, 2010.

Spude, Catherine Holder, *"That Fiend in Hell": Soapy Smith in Legend*, University of Oklahoma Press, 2012.

Swearengin, John, *Good Men, Bad Men, Lawmen, and a Few Rowdy Ladies*, self-published, 1991.

The editors of Time-Life Books, *The Gunfighters*, Time-Life Books, 1981.

The editors of *True West, True Tales and Amazing Legends of the Old West*, Clarkson Potter, 2005.

Vulich, Nick, *Shot All to Hell: Bad Ass Outlaws, Gunfighters, and Lawmen of the Old West*, Kindle Edition, Amazon e-book, 2016.

Wright, Mike, *What They Didn't Teach You About the Wild West*, Presidio, Novato, California, 2000.

Yeatman, Ted P., *Frank and Jesse James: The Story Behind the Legend*, Fall River Press, 2000.

Younger, Cole, *The Story of Cole Younger, by Himself*, The Hennenberry Company, 1903.

DISCOGRAPHY

Guy Clark and Waylon Jennings – "The Last Gunfighter Ballad" (2010)
Bob Dylan – *John Wesley Harding* (1967)
Lorne Greene – "Ringo" (45 rpm single, 1964)
Woody Guthrie – "Pretty Boy Floyd" (78 rpm, 1939) and "Jesse James" (78 rpm, 1944)
Dickson Hall – *Outlaws of the Old West* (1956, reissued by Bear Family in 2003)
Marty Robbins – *Gunfighter Ballads and Trail Songs* (1959)
Steve Tilston – *Of Moor and Mesa* (1992)
Tom Petty and the Heartbreakers – "Two Gunslingers" (1991)

Clark and Jennings' aging "last gunfighter" gets run down by a car. Petty's song is about gunslingers who hang up their holsters. Many of these outlaws, if they hadn't died early by gun or rope, would have lived to see automobiles and electric lights. Dickson Hall (born Floyd Sherman Riley) is an interesting character. His album has songs about most of the characters profiled in this book, including Jesse James, Billy the Kid, Belle Starr, The Dalton Brothers, Black Bart, and Johnny Ringo.

INDEX

JIM MOTAVALLI writes for the *New York Times*, The Wharton School at the University of Pennsylvania, *Barron's*, NPR's *Car Talk*, Autoblog, and others. He lectures frequently on environmental topics in the US and abroad. Motavalli is a two-time winner of the Global Media Award from the Population Institute, and hosts a radio program on WPKN-FM in Connecticut, with frequent guests and live music. He has two daughters, and lives with his wife in Fairfield, Connecticut.

ALSO BY JIM MOTAVALLI

The Real Dirt on America's Frontier Legends

High Voltage: The Fast Track to Plug in the Auto Industry

Naked in the Woods: Joseph Knowles and the History of Frontier Fakery

Earth Talk: Expert Answers to Everyday Questions About the Environment

Green Living: The E Magazine Handbook for Living Lightly on the Earth

Feeling the Heat: Dispatches from the Frontlines of Climate Change

Breaking Gridlock: Moving Toward Transportation That Works

Forward Drive: The Race to Build the Clean Car of the Future

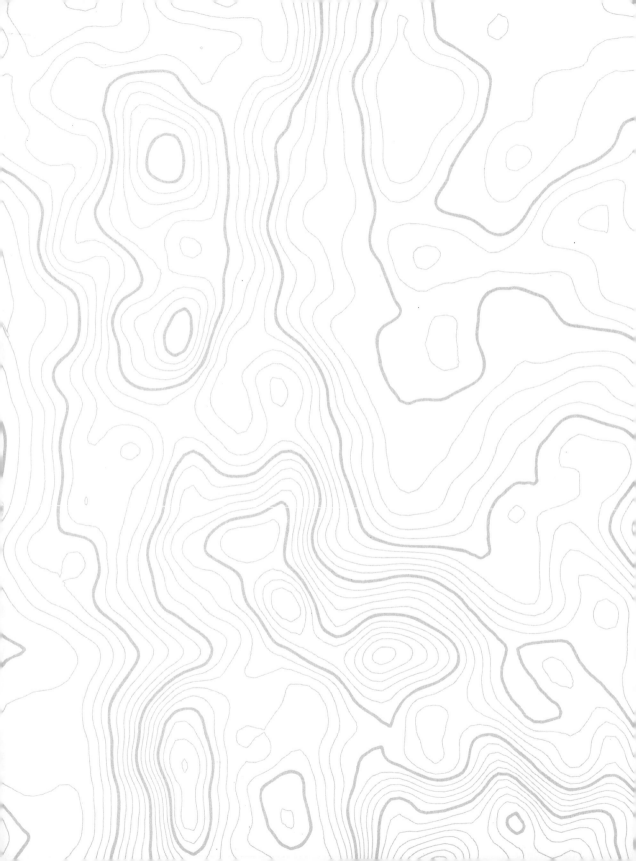